SECRETS TO PERSONAL AND
PROFESSIONAL EFFECTIVENESS

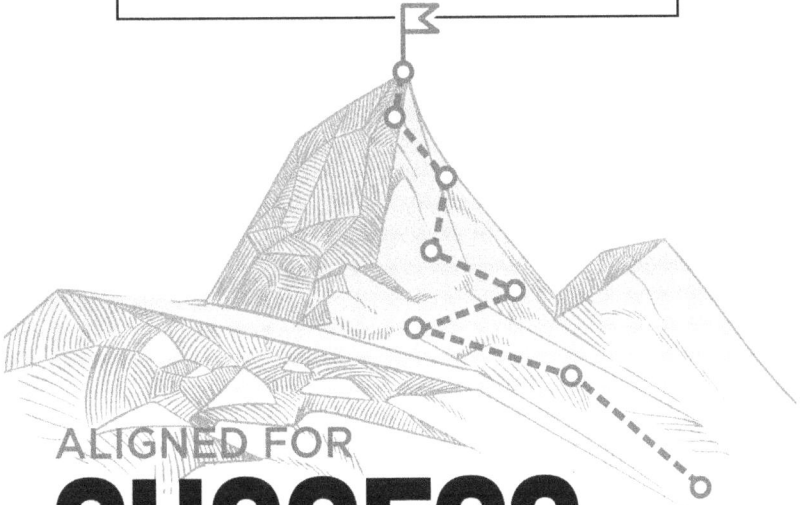

ALIGNED FOR

SUCCESS

EDITED BY **VAN MOODY**

Aligned for Success: Secrets to Personal and Professional Effectiveness
edited by Van Moody

copyright ©2019
ISBN: 978-1-950718-20-7
Printed in the United States of America

cover design by Martijn van Tilborgh
Aligned for Success is available in Amazon Kindle, Barnes & Noble Nook and Apple iBooks.

CONTENTS

INTRODUCTION

N O MATTER WHAT sphere of influence you lead in—a home, a business, a ministry, a nonprofit, or simply in your personal life—we all have a soul-level need for alignment. God designed us to be aligned with His truth in every aspect of our lives. The problem is, the troubles of this world and the attacks of the enemy throw us off balance. This book is about getting you back on the right track.

You may be experiencing lack of alignment in your finances. Maybe your organization feels out of control. Your health may be suffering because of a lack of time management. Maybe you're not entirely sure what alignment has to do with your walk with Christ in the first place. The following collection of thoughts from world-class business and ministry leaders paints a holistic picture of the essential nature of alignment for believers. If we're not aligned with God's Word, our teams, families, health—and, ultimately, our calling and legacy—will all suffer.

We hope you find enlightenment, inspiration, encouragement, and the push you need to step into alignment in a rejuvenating way through this book. Read each chapter with humility, and pray that the Holy Spirit would reveal to you where you've been out of alignment, so that He can lovingly restore you to wholeness. Indeed, only when we come into alignment with Him and His Word do we step into the true, abundant life we're meant to have in Jesus Christ.

chapter 1

ALIGNMENT AS A TEST FOR LEADERSHIP

VAN MOODY

A LIGNMENT IS ONE of the most essential components of leadership. In fact, you can't be an effective leader without it. When things aren't aligned in your life and leadership, they are sure to take a turn for the worse.

If you've driven for any length of time, you're familiar with this principle. A car that is out of alignment will pull in one direction. This lack of alignment severely hampers your ability to control the car, or to get where you're headed. Maybe you've also experienced misalignment in your home. When a door is not in line with its frame, it can't close properly. The home is exposed to cold air, inclement weather, and all manner of creatures from outside. Chiropractors exist to treat our bodies' malalignment, which causes pain. We see that, in all areas of life, alignment is critical to success.

I know a number of people with great potential who struggle with leadership because they are not aligned properly. Just like leadership, alignment begins in the heart. If you are not aligned properly, your influence—your leadership—will be minimal. To maximize your abilities, you need to have proper alignment. What does this mean practically? It means *leaders need to die to self.*

The greatest leader who ever lived is Jesus Christ. Nothing about Jesus' life was about him. His entire life is a picture of dying to self. His years on earth, His ministry, and everything He did was about others. Because He willingly died to self, His influence as a leader knows no end, and has absolutely no boundaries.

The Bible offers us another interesting leadership example in the Old Testament account of Elijah and Elisha. Elisha is Elijah's mentee and is perhaps best known for his desire to have a double portion of Elijah's anointing. In 2 Kings 2:9, Elijah asks Elisha, "Tell me, what can I do for you before I am taken from you?" Elisha replies, "Let me inherit a double portion of your spirit." Elisha wants to accomplish double the ministry—participate in double the miracles. Elijah performs *eight* miracles during his time of ministry. Elisha wants to perform *sixteen*. However, we see that

Elisha accomplishes only fifteen and dies one miracle short of his goal. Second Kings 13:20-21 reads:

Elisha died and was buried.

Now Moabite raiders used to enter the country every spring. Once while some Israelites were burying a man, suddenly they saw a band of raiders; so they threw the man's body into Elisha's tomb. When the body touched Elisha's bones, the man came to life and stood up on his feet.

Elisha *did* participate in sixteen miracles! The final miracle, which allowed him to accomplish his dream, did not happen until *after he died.* The greater things God wants to do in your life as a leader—the things you're called to accomplish—won't happen until after you die. But I'm not talking about a physical death; I'm talking about dying to self.

Elijah first noticed Elisha because of his heart to serve. Here we find another leadership principle: the way you start is the way you should live every day. Some leaders fall into, or inherit, an opportunity; but most leaders are given opportunity because they demonstrate a tenacity for serving others.

The lawyer fresh out of law school has the desire to work for a firm, so he starts as an associate. He works hard—he knows the partners are watching and evaluating his performance. The new lawyer is tenacious, and shows a strong desire to serve the firm's clients. Then, he gets promoted.

Likewise, the intern takes a position in order to learn the ropes and demonstrate to a company that she is worth their investment. If she puts all of her energy into serving the company's mission, she'll stand out and be offered a position. This tenacity and drive is essential for leaders, whether they're newly-minted or have decades of experience in their fields.

I had an opportunity to interact with some individuals at a leadership roundtable recently, and we talked about the global church Hillsong. What an amazing group of believers! God empowered Hillsong to make a tremendous, worldwide impact. These individuals shared their philosophy of identifying and promoting leaders within their body.

At Hillsong, leaders serve their way in, up, and out. They are noticed because they are tenaciously, passionately serving. Then, they are put into positions of leadership. They continue to serve with the same intentionality—don't miss this. This faithfulness gets them promoted to greater leadership opportunities, through which they continue to serve—the cycle continues. One leader's service may result in God leading them out of Hillsong and into another ministry. If so, this individual leaves, having served their way in, up, and out! All the while, these believers lead as they began—with tenacious service.

Let's go back to Elijah and Elisha. Look at 1 Kings 19:19–21:

So Elijah went from there and found Elisha son of Shaphat. He was plowing with twelve yoke of oxen, and he himself was driving the twelfth pair. Elijah went up to him and threw his cloak around him. Elisha then left his oxen and ran after Elijah. "Let me kiss my father and mother goodbye," he said, "and then I will come with you."
"Go back," Elijah replied. "What have I done to you?" So Elisha left him and went back. He took his yoke of oxen and slaughtered them. He burned the plowing equipment to cook the meat and gave it to the people, and they ate. Then he set out to follow Elijah and became his servant.

Elisha stood out because of his service. He was plowing, driving the twelfth pair of oxen himself. Elijah went up to Elisha and threw his cloak, his mantle, around him. The term "mantle" means something ample, powerful and wonderful. Elisha was about to get a greater opportunity than the one he had.

This opportunity came about because Elisha *started out* with service. Elijah saw this and said, "I want to give him a bigger opportunity." Then, he walked away. Why? Because he wanted to find out if Elisha would remain in the same posture. Elijah thought, "I see you serving *now*. I see that you're willing to die to self *now*. I see that it's not about you *now*. But will you stay in that posture?" In other words, would Elisha remain in alignment? Or, when greater opportunity came, would he make it all about himself? Throughout the rest of their journey, Elijah continually tested Elisha to find out, "Are you going to stay in alignment? Are you still willing to die to self?"

I know a number of leaders who start strong. They start serving. They start with great intentions. Then, they get greater opportunity, and it becomes about them. These leaders get out of alignment. The moment this happens, their influence significantly decreases.

Over more than 25 years of leadership in business and ministry, I've learned that these are the same tests all leaders have to pass to remain in alignment. These aren't tests that come only once; they are often cyclical. You have to stay vigilant. What's at stake in your alignment is your ability to win with people—to get your message across and to build a God-honoring legacy. So, what are these tests? How can you make sure you're in alignment, so that you continue to influence and win with people?

TEST #1: DIE TO PREVIOUS PRIORITIES

In order for Elisha to follow Elijah, he had to leave things behind: his home, his farm, and his family. He could not have both lives. He could not continue to plow with the oxen and serve Elijah at the same time. He had to die to his previous priorities.

Here's a practical, everyday example of dying to priorities: Let's say I come home from the grocery store, and walk into the kitchen with my hands full. My son is sitting at the table looking at his iPad. I say, "Can you help me get the rest of the groceries out of the car?" My son says, "I'm using my iPad right now." Essentially he's telling me, "This thing in my hand is preventing me from doing what my father is asking me to do."

The "thing in our hands" might not be bad; however, if it prevents us from doing what our father is asking, we have a problem. Humans do this often. Distractions prevent leaders from fully engaging with what matters. We must be fully present, and we can't do that if we're preoccupied with old priorities. Unless we choose to die to our previous priorities, our hands will always be full. We'll miss out on the greater opportunities God has placed right in front of us.

TEST #2: DIE TO YOUR PAST

Take a look at 2 Kings 2:1–6:

When the Lord was about to take Elijah up to heaven in a whirlwind, Elijah and Elisha were on their way from Gilgal. Elijah said to Elisha, "Stay here; the Lord has sent me to Bethel."

But Elisha said, "As surely as the Lord lives and as you live, I will not leave you." So they went down to Bethel.

The company of the prophets at Bethel came out to Elisha and asked, "Do you know that the Lord is going to take your master from you today?"

"Yes, I know," Elisha replied, "so be quiet."

Then Elijah said to him, "Stay here, Elisha; the Lord has sent me to Jericho."

And he replied, "As surely as the Lord lives and as you live, I will not leave you." So they went to Jericho.

The company of the prophets at Jericho went up to Elisha and asked him, "Do you know that the Lord is going to take your master from you today?"

"Yes, I know," he replied, "so be quiet."

Then Elijah said to him, "Stay here; the Lord has sent me to the Jordan."

And he replied, "As surely as the Lord lives and as you live, I will not leave you." So the two of them walked on.

Elijah *was* eventually taken up in a whirlwind, and Elisha allowed his mantle to fall onto himself. This is what allowed Elisha to begin his journey to the double portion. Let's look at the specific locations mentioned in this passage: they are significant. The first stop is Gilgal, which is an important place in Israel's history. Gilgal is the first place the nation of Israel entered as they occupy the Promised Land. In Joshua 5, we learn that, before the Israelites entered the Promised Land, God told Joshua to circumcise all the men.

The word Gilgal literally means a rolling, or rolling away. The place is called Gilgal because, through the act of circumcision, God said, "I've rolled away your past.

I've rolled away the reproach of Egypt." These people had spent 40 years wandering in the wilderness. They had a lot of traumatic past to roll away; but God did it. Gilgal served as the location of a sign that the Israelites were no longer to be focused on their past. From then onward, they were to focus on God, their present, and their future.

Elijah and Elisha began their journey in a place that memorializes the rolling away of the past. We see that, if you don't deal with your past, you won't be able to embrace your future. This is a challenge for many leaders who see their present through the lens of their past. Whenever this happens, leaders cannot win. They end up losing influence because they are unable to adapt to the needs of the present and the future.

You must die to your past, both its good and bad elements. You can't rest on your laurels; nor can you obsess over your past mistakes. One of my favorite poems is "The Man in the Arena," which is an excerpt of a speech from Theodore Roosevelt. The poem states that, regardless of how many times you've messed up, the victory belongs to the person who presses forward and continues to fight for what's in front of them—*not* what's behind them.

TEST #3: DIE TO YOUR PASSIONS

The story continues, "So they went down to Bethel." Jacob named Bethel after he had a powerful encounter with God. He dreamed of a stairway to heaven, above which the Lord was standing. When Jacob woke, he named the place Bethel, which means "House of God." Later, he returned and built an altar there, and God spoke to him. Much later, the Israelites kept the ark of the covenant in Bethel.

If we want to have powerful encounters with God, we can't let our passions get in the way. Instead, we must be passionate about God and what He wants. We must choose God's passions over our own, and that requires first dying to our passions.

One of my favorite examples of this principle is the leader Truett Cathy. I grew up in Atlanta, where Chick-Fil-A is an institution. Chick-Fil-A was founded in Atlanta, but it has since become a huge brand, with restaurants all over the nation. The blessing and favor on this franchise exist because Cathy died to his own passions and made his passion for God his primary focus.

When Cathy started Chick-fil-A, people laughed at him. They told him he would never be successful. Why? Because, to everybody else, it seemed ludicrous to be closed on Sunday. Yet Cathy built his company on the foundational value that the Sabbath matters. His relationship with the Lord was more important than his business. He put his passion for the Lord ahead of his passion for money and success. He began his franchise with a promise to the Lord: "My passion for You, and what You want me to do, will always be number one." Look what God has done over the years! God has blessed the Chick-Fil-A franchise in a phenomenal way.

You cannot be in love with God and in love with yourself at the same time. Likewise, you can't be in love with God and in love with your passions at the same time. Jesus tells us that we can't serve, or love, two masters. We will end up loving one and hating the other. If you love God more than your passions, you will be an effective leader. If you love your passions more than God, there will always be a problem with your effectiveness.

TEST #4: DIE TO YOUR POWER

This is a hard one for leaders. The next stop on Elijah and Elisha's journey was Jericho. When the Israelites entered the Promised Land, Jericho was the site of their first battle; and this proved to be no ordinary skirmish.

The walls around the city of Jericho were high, strong, and fortified. God gave the Israelites a weird battle strategy, to say the least. He didn't tell them to tear down the walls or scale them; He told them to march around them blowing trumpets. Hearing this plan, one might ask, "How in the world were they going to win *that way*?" But this is exactly God's point. They *couldn't* win that way—not on their own power. God was going to win it with His power.

God told them to march and blow trumpets to ensure that they knew He was the powerful One—that He would win the battle for them. The Israelites wouldn't rely on themselves. They would rely on God. This is difficult for leaders to do. When problems arise, we often go into "fix-it mode." We count on our degrees and our ingenuity, thinking that these will make the difference. At the end of the day, they don't. When it really counts, what makes the difference is relying on the Lord.

I know too many leaders who end up tired, burnt out, and frustrated because they think, "How am *I* going to do this?" The most important thing you can do as a leader is to rely on God. You need to be in communion with Him daily, regardless of your position. You will need His help every hour, because you will encounter challenges that are bigger than you. God has already gone before you and provided the solution. Unless we tap into His plan, we will end up tired, burnt out, and frustrated, too.

TEST #5: BE WILLING TO TRANSITION

The final test for Elisha came at their final stop: the Jordan River.

The Jordan River is significant because, throughout Scripture, it represents transition from death to new life. Jesus was baptized in the Jordan; upon rising, He began His earthly ministry. The nation of Israel had to cross the Jordan in order to transition from the wilderness to the Promised Land. Elijah struck the Jordan with his cloak, and it parted. After Elijah was taken up with the whirlwind, Elisha did the same thing, to the same effect. This prompted onlookers to say, "The spirit of Elijah is resting on Elisha." At the Jordan, Elisha transitioned from student to prophet—from disciple to leader.

If we are to lead effectively, we must be willing to walk through, cross over, and submit to the transitions God has for us. Die to your old self, put on the new man, and just watch what God does.

When you pass all these tests, you will be in alignment. Your heart will be in the right place: after God. God will be able to use you. We must stay in this alignment continually, which means staying in constant contact with Him. If you find yourself getting a bit out of alignment, pause, and allow God to straighten you out, so that you can continue giving Him your best.

chapter 2

KEYS TO LEADERSHIP SUCCESS

NICOLE LABEACH

N MY EXPERIENCE, I've worked with a spectrum of leaders: athletes, entertainers, pastors, vice presidents, and C-Suite executives. Throughout the years, I've discovered that there are six critical components to being aligned for leadership success. Let's take a look at each one of them in detail.

1. CONGRUENCE WITH GOD'S VIEW OF YOU

It's difficult to lead if you have a distorted understanding of your own identity and value. Yet so many leaders struggle to see themselves the way God sees them.

God sees us as He created us—who we are in Him. But things happen in our lives that distort how we see ourselves. Eventually, our picture doesn't match up with God's. We behave as though our self-view is the absolute truth about who we are. But who we are never truly changes.

Negative things happen to good people, but these events don't have the power to rewrite who we are. They can't mutate our DNA. Sure, negative events are parts of our story; and they can be a page in it. However, these challenges don't get to take over the story and determine how it ends. They don't redefine who we are. We need to make sure we're not giving circumstances the opportunity to define us, and thereby granting them more power than they have. Over and over, I've seen leaders give events the power to create a debilitating narrative. The objective is to move away from the bad things that have happened, and back toward the person God sees you to be. You can do this, because you have the power of the pen.

We have the power to write our own narratives. The man who thinks he can't, as well as the man who thinks he can, are both right. The first man sees things that have happened, decides his options are limited—that he's not deserving of success—and surrenders his pen to his circumstances. The second man uses things that have happened to inform his narrative, but he still sees all the opportunities. He realizes he has a powerful position of possibility.

As a leader, you have the opportunity to pick up your pen and say, "You know what? Bad things have happened; but I decide how I see those things, because my DNA and my make-up are still good. Nothing that's happened has the power to shift who I am. It's part of my story, but it's not my definition."

Stay connected to God's view of you. From that connection, amazing things will happen.

2. VISION AND VISIBILITY

Vision is not about *feasibility*; it's about *visibility*.

Before anyone walked on the moon, someone had to envision someone walking on the moon. Before all the arguments about the difficulties, the technology, and the specifics, there was a vision. Vision and visibility came first. Feasibility came later. Somebody had to visually connect with the possibility of a man on the moon to start the conversation of how he might get up there.

Often, we have inappropriate alignment conversations. As a leader, you have to see your vision clearly so you can articulate it to others. When you're focused on engineering your vision, to bring in the question of feasibility only muddies the water. It short-circuits your ability to see your vision clearly. Don't think about hearing "No" or "You can't." Those are premature questions. Don't think about how much money you have available for the vision. Fear will only distort your vision by presenting to your mind all the things that *could become* road blocks, but aren't yet.

The objective, then, is to think about your vision in a perfect scenario. At this point, only focus on what you can see—what you can give yourself permission to imagine. Clearly commit to seeing the vision. Visualize it. Write it down. This ensures that, when you *do* bring feasibility into the conversation, it won't change the vision. If you don't write your vision down, it can gradually become less than it was.

Proper vision envisioning is tied to being in alignment with your identity in Christ. If you're limited by a negative self-view, your vision will suffer, and you'll become intimidated by matters of feasibility. On the flip side, when you're in congruence with how God sees you, you have the audacity to think that a man can walk on the moon. You're not worried about how he'll breathe, or what he'll wear. You're just imagining the possibilities. From this foundation, you begin to visualize what that might look like, and begin to add the specific components based on your vision.

Before we get too far down that line of thought, let's start intentionally building our team.

3. IDENTIFY YOUR KEY PLAYERS
Who are your drivers?
As a leader, you need to identify those who will get behind your vision and drive it. These are people with the knowledge, capacity, and competence to drive your cause across the finish line. Who are these drivers for you?

Who are your doers?

Next, consider who will do the work. You've got a vision. You're in congruence with how God sees you, so you're not shaking at the knees or betraying the vision. You know exactly what you're going for, but now you've got to implement and execute. So who are your doers?

Who are your access providers?

Access providers are people who open doors for you. Some will only crack a door open; some will pull doors open so wide that you can somersault through them. Some are going to connect you with their network. Some will make introductions for you. Who are these people in your world?

Who are your donors?

You'll need people who can donate to and invest in your cause. They can help you make the incremental steps forward that need to be made. Who might these donors be for you?

Who are your coaches and accountability partners?

When Tiger Woods was in his prime, he had nine coaches. Most of us can understand that—after all, he was the best in the world. One move, one pattern, one false alignment of his body could make the difference between winning a championship and losing a championship. Who are your accountability partners? Who will tell you the truth and hold you accountable to what you've said you are going to accomplish?

Who are your mentors?

Who's already been down the road you're traveling on? Mentors have great vantage points, and can tell you what to look out for and how to position yourself to make the best moves. Whom can you ask to mentor you?

Who are your encouragers?

Encouragers love you no matter what. They see the best in you, and want what's best for you. These individuals will speak positivity to you, especially during the critical times when you really need it. Whom do you know who is an encourager?

Who are your experts?

You also need subject matter experts to help you manifest your vision. These people help during the midst of the feasibility conversations. You don't want to have these talks by yourself; you need others involved who can inform you, help you understand what to watch for, and advise you about what questions to ask.

Who are your customers?

Who are your end users and customers? You have to know whom you aim to serve with your vision. Of course, as you move down the road, more customers and end users may jump on the bandwagon. But in the beginning, be clear about whom your vision is going to serve. Think about what's important to these people. Give your focus to your ideal customer, and your vision will achieve its maximum effectiveness.

In every team, there are cuts. Not everyone can make the team. So in order to be aligned for success, you need to know who your team is, know the rules of the team, know what position each person plays, and be clear about who is and who isn't on your team. This may require you to make some changes. For this reason, it's important to be comfortable with the change-making process.

4. ENGAGE IN CHANGE

A leader needs to be comfortable with change. At some point, he or she will go through change, lead others through it, or both.

Kurt Lewin is considered by many to be the father of organizational psychology. Many years ago, he created a model of change. Lewin says that you've got to unfreeze it, change it, and then refreeze it.

Think of an ice cube. If you want to change the content of the ice cube, you first have to melt it. Then, you can mix it with something and refreeze it. If you want to change the shape of the ice cube, the same principle applies. You have to melt it, change the shape of the container, and refreeze it.

The same principle applies to leadership. If you have a vision of putting a man on the moon, you must have a conversation about what needs to change. You first need to "unfreeze" the current mindset around the idea, modify it to allow for your vision, and then refreeze the mindset.

You may be thinking, "You know, there *are* some mind-sets I need to change to push my vision forward." Great! So, what do you need to "melt"? What do you have to let go of first? What old ways of thinking do you need to shift? Once you've melted these old mindsets, you must change them. For this step, ask yourself these questions: What do you need to do differently? What do you need to do better? What do you need to start, or stop, doing? After you've made these changes, you can reinforce the change and "freeze" it, so that it becomes the new way of pursuing the vision.

What do you need to melt away? How can you prepare people for this process? What do you need to put in place, and how do you need to refreeze things? As a leader, you need to be aligned in a power stance. One of the best ways to get and maintain this stance is to ask these questions. Questions lead to opportunities to make strategic moves.

So, you begin by making sure your view of yourself is congruent with God's view of you. This helps you to have a clear vision that extends to the heights it deserves. Then identify who your key players are—who will help you manifest the vision and facilitate necessary change. Next, you'll need to ask some questions.

5. ASK THE CRITICAL QUESTIONS

A vision is for the future. As such, vision always requires change. And change requires asking the necessary questions.

What is my ask?

You may be surprised at how many leaders get into a room with an expert, donor, or door opener...and don't know what to ask for. The person probably can't grant your request unless you communicate it. Similarly, if you want someone on your team, you need to ask them to join, and explain the role you want them to play.

What do I need to know and learn?

When you get into a sticky situation, you don't want to be oblivious. You want to be sharp—to have the knowledge necessary to make decisions that cut through the stickiness. It is important that you work to acquire this knowledge *before* you need it.

What are the critical action points in my plan?

Leaders have to work backward from the vision. If vision is the end, what are the incremental points that lead up to its fulfillment? Identify these markers, and lay them out so that you don't go off course.

What strategy should I employ?

You need to have a plan and a strategy. How will you meet your critical action points? How will you utilize your team and other resources to their fullest potential? The answers to these questions will determine your strategy.

What is my timeline?

Leaders without a schedule often never reach their destination. Create a working timeline, and then stick to it. Things will happen; you will have to revise the timeline; but this doesn't mean you should abandon it altogether. A timeline keeps you accountable to your goals, and those markers of success you set up earlier.

What processes should I employ?

As a leader, you know how vital processes and systems are. So what systems are you putting in place to help you deliver positive outcomes? This is one of the most essential elements of seeing your vision come to life.

What am I willing to try?

Are you willing to unfreeze some of your old ways of doing things so that new ways can come into play? Is there something you need to stop doing, or something you need to start?

What matters most to my team members?

Be clear on the position in which you've placed your teammates. Can they be effective there? Have you put them where *you* want them without their agreement? Do they even understand your vision? Sometimes, you'll find that someone has more expertise, or connections, than you realized. A team member may be waiting to say, "I'm more than a donor; I'm also a door opener. I can help you access other relationships." Don't overlook these possibilities by underestimating those around you.

As you're answering these questions, stay engaged with your team. You're not a leader if no one is following you. Stay present. Look around and take notice of how *they* are experiencing the journey. Then, ask yourself what you can do to make it easier for them: how can you make it meaningful, so that they keep showing up and giving you their best?

If you've done all of this, then you see yourself the way God sees you. You've got the vision, and it makes sense to you. You've got your key players, and you've figured out their positioning. You're ready for change. You're activating and leveraging change. You've asked the critical questions, and you've gotten the important answers. Now what? It's critical to ask the right questions and get answers; but what's even more critical is doing something with the answers you've received. *You have to press play.*

6. MOVE

You can't move toward success if you're unwilling. You have to move based on the answers you've discovered. You can't deliberate indefinitely. You've got to use some verbs—some actions.

Many times, leaders say to me, "This is the decision. Hopefully, it's the right one." I tell them, "Well, I don't know if it is or not. Let's find out. And if we find out that it's not the right decision, we'll make a different one." But we can't just keep thinking about it forever. Standing still won't tell us anything; moving will tell us whether we're moving down the right path or the wrong path.

Passivity is a myth—especially for leaders. Something is always happening, even if *you're* not doing anything.

It's better to make an informed decision, and let it move you forward.

Paul Batalden from Dartmouth once said, "Every system is perfectly designed to get the result that it gets." I think this is brilliant. If you're not getting the result you want, it's because the system you have in place is not designed to get you the desired result. Hence, you need to make a change. Put a system in place, have processes, and tweak the system until you get the outcome you want.

These six components work in synergy to make you a well-aligned, effective, powerful leader. You will know who you are through God's eyes, and you will have the vision God wants you to have. You will surround yourself with a team perfectly equipped to execute your vision. You will be ready, willing, and able to change. You will be courageous in asking the right questions, and you will be brave in acting on the answers you discover. *That* is proper alignment!

chapter 3

CREATING ATMOSPHERES OF ALIGNMENT

MYESHA CHANEY

L EADERSHIP ALIGNMENT HAS been heavily researched and discussed throughout multiple fields. If you were to do an internet search right now, you'd find a wealth of information on the topic. I want to zero in on the heart level of alignment. At the core, alignment in any organization comes about through the cooperation of other people. My focus is cultivating environments that foster alignment in all spheres of life—in your business, your home, your ministry, and amongst your staff.

God made us relational beings. We need to know how to motivate people: what to do; what to say; how to go about creating communities aligned with our vision.

If we do that, we'll have people on the bus, in the right seats, passionately doing their part to make God's calling for us come to pass.

With this goal in mind, I invite you to consider the needs and desires of the people you're leading—those in your life and under your care. I've been deeply influenced by a book called *The Seven Desires of Every Heart* by Mark and Debra Laaser, and I want to share some of their principles as they relate to leadership alignment.

People have deep desires. Sometimes, these desires are hidden and not readily accessible. People don't always put words to them. Still, as long as we attempt to meet the needs of those on our team, our organizations can be aligned, and that alignment leads to success. When we care for those under us we help them get on board and move in the right direction. This also honors God. After all, God put our desires within us in the first place! When we're born, and throughout our childhood, these desires need to be met. If they aren't, we find unhealthy ways to fulfill them later in life.

Of course, when we try to meet others' needs, we will sometimes meet resistance. It can cause a bit of upheaval. There are contrary people who think they know what's best, and those who simply want to fight. Some people bring their baggage with them. Regardless of how difficult some team members can be, each of the people you work with has deep, God-planted needs to be met. As their leader, you have an opportunity there to meet some of those deep needs.

Humans have seven universal desires. You can use this information for self-growth, as well as in application for the people in your life. Ultimate fulfillment in life is the result of having these desires met, as well as the opportunity to meet them in others. When these key desires are fulfilled, people experience deeper and fuller relationship with God and others. Content, fulfilled human beings work with all that's in their hearts, and they are the most productive type of people.

DESIRE #1: EVERYONE DESIRES TO BE HEARD AND UNDERSTOOD.

Some people in your organization are living according to false narratives. They don't speak up because they believe they are not worthy of being heard, or that they'd be a bother. They think their needs are too much for others. Sometimes, they don't even *know* that they have a desire to be heard. However, everyone has the desire to be heard. *Everyone.*

As leaders, we must find ways to truly listen and understand the thoughts and feelings of others. Practically, this can look like opening up the floor during the last ten minutes of a meeting, or starting a suggestion box. No matter what it looks like, listening is essential. When we listen to others, we confirm that their opinions are worthy of being heard—worthy of our time. Our act of listening communicates that what they say is valuable. If you want to cultivate alignment in your organization, begin listening. Allow people to be heard and understood.

DESIRE #2: EVERYONE DESIRES TO BE AFFIRMED.

Humans want to know that somebody believes in us—someone approves of who we are and what we do. Affirmation tells us that we're doing well, and to keep it up. It's somebody who says, "Go! Go! You're going in the right direction! Keep going! I see what you're doing. It's good! Keep up the good work." Tragically, many people not only lack affirmation, but are consistently criticized and put down. Criticism simply says, "You messed up." It's no wonder that heavily criticized people lose sight of what they're doing and why.

Our need for affirmation is so great that, sometimes, we refuse to try new things. We're scared because we don't want to look foolish. We don't want people to judge and criticize us. It's difficult to lead those struggling with such things. You're trying to feed them a vision, and it seems they're just not getting it. They aren't moving forward, and you think, *I'm trying to do what God has put in me. I'm trying to take this organization to the next level. What's going on?* What's going on is that people are operating out of fear of failure because they haven't had their need for affirmation met. They're living by a false narrative that says they can't do it.

When someone wrestles with their ability to be accepted, and questions the value of their contributions, they get out of alignment. Some strive for perfection, working double or triple overtime to convince others they're worthy. Some people will lie to avoid disappointing their leader. They would rather be affirmed in their lie than tell a difficult truth. But as a leader, you need to hear the difficult truths, and you need people to be healthy and brave enough to tell you the truth.

All of these issues are huge blocks to true alignment. You can bring things into alignment by making sure everyone receives affirmation. Speak encouraging words over people: "You're doing well. You are worthy. Thank you for being here. Your work makes a difference." When was the last time you affirmed somebody in your organization? Remember, the Bible tells us to encourage one another daily—to spur one another on toward love and good deeds.

We need to remember that we're working with *people*—individual souls with individual needs. They are not robots or worker bees. Every vision that comes to pass, every great leader who emerges, and every great exploit for God requires a community. In that community, there are people who long to be affirmed.

DESIRE #3: EVERYONE DESIRES TO BE BLESSED.

We all want to be blessed. Blessing is about who we are, because blessing is an affirmation of who we are.

As we said above, all humans want to know that they are enough.

When we're blessed, we see that we're special in somebody's eyes. I remember going to retreats where I would wait in line to be blessed; I wanted somebody to see something in me and bless me. When someone else speaks a blessing over you, it brings light to something you can't see in yourself. It's a huge part of what we give to one another in community. People want to know that they're enough, and when we're blessed, we don't have to perform for that love; we're loved and accepted for who we are. Practically, this may look like small tokens of appreciation. It may mean unexpected words of blessing—saying, "I bless you today" over those in your life.

How often are we taking advantage of moments to bless people? How often are we doing things for them that weren't expected or earned? You never know—the very words you speak as a blessing may contradict the false narrative they're believing in that moment. They may be sitting in your staff meeting thinking, *I can't do anything right.* But when you speak words of life over them, they see themselves the way you see them; the way God sees them.

Maybe you have someone in your ministry whom you want to call on to take a different post. They're thinking, "I'm not worthy to receive a blessing. Is there something wrong with me? I need to work harder to get more people to bless me. I have to do more." But when you come alongside them, look at them, and say, "Wow, you're worthy," it changes everything for that person.

Some people believe that giving and receiving blessing is based on performance. This causes them to work harder, but work in itself doesn't bring blessing. Blessing is not about what we do; it's about who we are. The desire to be blessed may be our deepest, most primal need. We need to know that if everything else—our accomplishments, ministry posts, honors, possessions, all of it—were stripped away, we would still be loved. Think of the top earner in your business: that person who's always doing their best. Believe it or not, they are the person who probably most needs to hear these words: "Even if you fail, you're still loved and accepted here."

Think about the last thirty days. When have you felt blessed? When have you heard words of blessing—and when have you given them to others? You may not see these desires on the surface, but they're there. The moment you meet that need, you'll have people saying, "Wherever you're taking us, we want to go. We follow your leadership. We follow your vision."

DESIRE #4: EVERYONE DESIRES TO FEEL SAFE AND SECURE.

Human beings want to be materially secure. We want to know that we have food, a place to live, and money to support ourselves. We also yearn for relational security—to know that those around us are reliable and caring toward us. Lastly, we want to be spiritually secure. We want to know that God is not the kind of God who's going to pull the rug out from under us. We want to feel safe—in our jobs, ministry positions, and in our service to God.

Feeling safe and secure means being free from fear and anxiety. Some people live with angst—they come to your team with financial issues, trauma, or other challenges, which cause them constant anxiety and fear. These people are pulled out of alignment because they don't feel that basic sense of security. Their desire isn't being met. It's helpful for us as leaders to understand this desire so we can do something about it.

When someone feels secure, it results in forgiveness of self and others. It brings a freedom that allows for risk-taking, generosity, and stepping out in ways that enhance the organization or family. People who feel free are more likely to give to and bless others. And once we feel free, we're more likely to express our other needs and desires, as well.

Still, there are false narratives in play. Some people believe they are alone in this world—that they are alone in caring for themselves, and that they have the ability to do so without help. These people keep their superhero capes on around the clock, and tell themselves that they can do anything. Sometimes they're extremely controlling, because they believe that controlling others will provide the sense of security they're sorely lacking. As leaders, we can help to reshape these false narratives by doing our part to meet their desire. We can help provide safety and security to those who are, secretly or not secretly, afraid.

When you step into a new leadership role, especially in ministry, it's easy to make wide, sweeping changes: "We're going left now! We're going to burn up everything we've been doing and start fresh!" This can cause tremendous anxiety for those you're leading. After all, they felt safe and secure in their previous roles, traditions, and environments. When you want to go in a different direction, it matters how you present it. Leaders need to make changes; but if these changes take away security for people, we need to find other ways to continue meeting that desire.

DESIRE #5: EVERYONE DESIRES TO BE TOUCHED.

The University of North Carolina found that people who hug regularly have a lower risk of heart disease. You might be able to save on your insurance premiums by allowing people to embrace each other.

We never outgrow the need for touch. Touch is critical to our wellbeing and our sense of self in the world. Think about your last week. How many people gave you a hug or a handshake? How did that make you feel? Even people who are less comfortable being touched still have a desire to be touched—just in the ways with which they are comfortable. It's also worth noting that we should always ask permission before embracing someone.

Jesus demonstrated the healing power of touch. He touched the lepers: the unclean. He knew that they desperately needed this, perhaps more than anyone else in their society. Our souls need the healing that comes through touch—even if it's just a hand on a shoulder that communicates, "I'm with you."

DESIRE #6: EVERYONE DESIRES TO BE CHOSEN.

I don't know how many times I've been overlooked, so this desire in particular resonates with me. In past years, I tried out for basketball. Most of the time, I didn't get picked because I was 5'1". That was a terrible feeling. On the flip side, when I think about the times I *have* been chosen—"I want you to be at my wedding"; "I would like you to participate in my event"; "Out of all the others, I choose your songs to play in the morning"—it's nothing short of heartwarming.

We all have the desire to be in a special relationship. Think about a time in the past when you've chosen someone. How did they react? Now, think of a time when someone chose you. What was your response? Did you felt special, accepted, and desired? In our environments, we have opportunities to cultivate this practice of choosing people. When we see the value in someone and say to them, "I'd like for you to be a part of this team. I pick you, out of everybody else, to step up and lead," we're sending a message congruent with God's truth about who we are.

You never know the effect your efforts will have. You may be the one to challenge someone's false narrative. Someone may believe they're not enough; they're not lovable; they're not as good as others; they're nobody, and no one will choose them. Then, you come alongside them and say, "You. I pick *you*." Pick people to serve in certain capacities. Pick them to lead. Just choose them. There are people waiting to be chosen, and this is a simple gift you can give them.

DESIRE #7: EVERYONE DESIRES TO BE INCLUDED.

We have an innate desire to be included in fellowship, with God and with other people. We want someone to involve us; we want to belong. This is one of the first desires awakened by our parents. Belonging is key. It's central to who we are.

There are people in your sphere of influence who want to be part of something great. Let's make that happen for them. They're more likely to cooperate, to be aligned, to do their part, when they feel they're included. The more we involve them, the better. Belonging is the foundation of self-esteem and trust. Within community, we feel that we're not alone. We have a sense of wellbeing. The desire to be included starts with a desire, in our soul, to belong to family.

So, how well are we cultivating family? How included do we feel, and how included do we make others feel? These questions apply to the families in our churches, clubs, organizations, and neighborhoods. It's a free gift to others to say, "Come on in, Johnny! Yeah, we've been waiting for you. We'd love for you to be a part of this." It's about extending yourself to reach people and bring them into a closer sense of community.

Somebody might think, *Nobody wants me. Nobody sees me. No one accepts me. I'm overlooked. I'm one of so many members.* We have an ability to meet their desire, simply by extending our hand and saying, "I want you to be included in this decision-making process. I value your opinion. I want your feedback about how we might move forward." It's a way of seeing the value they add, and acknowledging that their deepest desire is to be included. It doesn't matter where we are, or what position we hold. Everyone can do this.

Knowing these seven desires gives us an amazing opportunity to love people deeply. We can connect with them, and see God use this to foster environments for alignment. Alignment, of course, leads to success. I encourage you to find ways in your own life to love people for who they are, and to remember that, primarily, they want to be loved.

Sometimes, by thinking about our own desires, we can better meet the desires of others. What do you really want? You want your voice to be heard. You want to be affirmed and blessed. You want to feel safe and secure, knowing everything will be okay on all fronts. You want that gentle embrace from someone who cares. You want to be chosen and included. You want to feel like you belong. None of this is complicated.

Seeing, and meeting, people's desires will be life-changing for you. It will cultivate an environment of alignment. Perhaps most importantly, it will have a profound effect on those you lead. You might help someone realize their destiny. You might change what happens when someone leaves your organization, or when your child leaves home and goes to college. These people might think, *I remember this place, because I always felt included,* or, *I remember that boss, because he really believed in me.*

Daily, we have an opportunity to love and affirm people right where they are. We have an opportunity to see our vision come to pass in ways we didn't think possible, with everyone in the right seat, doing what they've been called to do. And then, we get the benefit of life transformation. With all these desires being met, there's nothing our churches, our businesses, our ministries, and our families can't do.

chapter 4

IDENTITY ALIGNMENT

WAYNE CHANEY

WOULD LIKE TO FOCUS on one foundational aspect of alignment that affects every area of our lives: identity.

I have a friend who has run almost every marathon in North America. At one point, his body began to give him problems. The pain started in his ankle, moved to his knee, to his hip, and eventually, to his back. This friend visited several specialists, bandaged his ankle, and got a knee brace and a back brace. However, he couldn't do much for his hip. He had to be sidelined because he couldn't figure out what was going on inside his body. Finally, one of the specialists realized that his pelvis was slightly tilted. This small misalignment was throwing off his entire skeletal structure. Once they aligned his pelvis, the rest of his body fell into order, and he was able to get rid of the bandage and braces and get back to work.

So many of us in ministry or business have a God-given leadership ability and are driven to lead. Yet we're on the verge of falling apart, because there's a bit of misalignment somewhere in our lives. James Lawrence's book, *Growing Leaders: Reflections on Leadership, Life, and Jesus,* really captures the misalignment so many leaders find themselves lured into. Lawrence calls it the "cycle of grief." He states that this cycle begins with achievement, moves to identity, continues to drivenness, and finally ends with acceptance. This is a pattern that continues perpetually in the lives of many leaders.

The negative cycle begins when we achieve something that provides us with a sense of identity. Our own significance then becomes dependent on what was achieved; so, of course, we try to achieve more. This brings us to drivenness. We're driven to achieve more and more in order to make ourselves acceptable, both to others and ourselves. Acceptance is a temporary, fragile state—it never lasts long. When it's over, we start the cycle again, with the end goal of feeling that acceptance once more. Around and around we go, trying to achieve more and more, until we find ourselves miserable—burned out, injured, exhausted, and confused about who we are and how we got here.

My purpose in writing this chapter is to make sure you know how to have alignment in the area of your identity. When you have the right perspective on identity, you won't slip into this perpetual cycle of grief. We want more than effectiveness and results—as leaders, we want longevity. We find the best pattern for longevity in Luke chapter 3. During Jesus' baptism, God speaks a word over the life of His Son.

Before we focus on *what* God says, let's look at *when* He says it. Before Jesus begins His earthly ministry; before He performs any miracles; before He has raised anyone from the dead, opened any blind eyes, or turned water into wine—this is when God speaks these earth-shaking words over His Son: "This is My Son, whom I love. In Him I am well pleased." In dramatic fashion, the heavens open, and the Father declares this absolute truth as the Holy Spirit descends on Jesus in the form of a dove.

Try to hear these words for yourself. "This is My son (daughter) whom I love. In him (her) I am well pleased."

Notice what's packed into these words. First, we see the pleasure of the Father spoken over His child. God lavishes His love on His Son before there is any performance to astound the world. So many of us need to take the time to feel—to just absorb—God's pleasure in us. Experience the love of the Father, detached from anything you will ever accomplish. God's love is not attached to what we *do*. There is nothing we can do to make God love us any more or any less. We need to carry this reality with us as we do ministry, but also in our workplace and our homes. The pleasure and love of the Father must be our anchor as we lead.

Now let's look at *what* He says. God's words establish Jesus' identity: "You are My Son." *You*, dear reader, are also God's child. This is your identity. This is who you are. You are *not* what you're able to accomplish, your intelligence, your appearance, your location, or your family. None of these things should fuel your behavior or your sense of worth.

I've found that when my sense of worth is placed in what I can do, there's a shift the moment that I can't do it anymore. My stress mounts, because I'm losing my sense of identity. I become unpinned from my foundation. Similarly, if I find my sense of worth in my intelligence, the moment I don't have the answers, my sense of self-worth goes down the tube. When my sense of self is connected to the important people I know, the moment the fabric of one of those relationships begins to unravel, my fortitude unravels with it.

It is vitally important to receive the love, affirmation, and pleasure of the Father. We need to make sure our identity is not tied to what we're able to do for God. I love that God speaks these words over Jesus as He is being baptized—not after He does all His greatest miracles. It's important that we establish our identity in

God and learn, on a daily basis, what it means to be a true son or daughter of the Most High.

Particularly in the Western world, we're defined by what we do—and we do a lot. When you sit down on a plane, the first thing the person next to you asks is, "What do you do for a living?" Why? We value accomplishment. We place a high premium on activity; however, very little of it is associated with who we really are at our core. If who we are isn't firmly established, it's like having a "tilted pelvis" that affects every other part of our life.

Sometimes we celebrate people because of their drivenness or accomplishments, not knowing they're one step away from self-sabotage—or even suicide. There are stress fractures under all that they've built, because their identity is tied to everything *but* the fact that they are a son or a daughter of God.

Once Jesus is baptized, the Spirit leads Him into the wilderness, where He is tempted by Satan. The *first* thing Satan does is attack Jesus' identity. God says, "This is My Son." The devil says, "*If* you are the Son of God," trying to plant seeds of doubt in Jesus' mind. Then the devil tries to link Jesus' identity with His activity: "If you are the Son of God, turn that stone into bread." *If you are really the Son of God, prove it by doing something.* What a lie! Long before James Lawrence wrote his book, the devil tried to bring Jesus into the cycle of grief that so many leaders face today.

Now, most people won't go into a literal wilderness to do a 40-day fast. I did a 40-day fast once, and I pray that God never calls me to do that again. It was not easy! Whether or not we ever do these things, each of us *will* find ourselves in some type of wilderness—a difficult area that forces us to lean on God and find our identity as His child.

Ask yourself this question: "What shapes my identity?" Some men find it in physical prowess—by how much they can bench and how big their biceps are. Some women find it in physical beauty. Some find identity in personal relationships—in marriages and parenthood. And sometimes, we glean our identity from others who've influenced us. Maybe your father was a Godly example, and you followed in his footsteps. Or maybe you had an uncle who was a player, so you find your identity in how many people are attracted to you. In ministry, our identity can become associated with how many members we have; so, to have a sense of worth, we have to keep membership high. In the workplace, your identity can be associated with your job title. If you were to lose your job tomorrow, your sense of esteem would go with it. We associate our identity with these external things, and the game—the cycle—continues to go on.

It's extremely easy to lose sight of the fact that our identity is in who God says we are—in the fact that we are his children. In the wilderness, Satan tempts Jesus in every way in which we, as leaders, are tempted. He says, "Turn these stones into bread," trying to entice the lust of the flesh. He says, "Bow down to me, and I'll give you everything your eyes can see," trying to entice the lust of the eyes. And he says, "You jump from the pinnacle of the temple, and God will command His angels concerning you. They will bear you up in their arms that your foot will not be dashed against the stones," trying to entice the pride of life.

The lust of the flesh includes the temptation to feel physical pleasure. The lust of the eyes includes the things that make us long for *more*. This lust makes us covet things we don't need. The pride of life appeals to our own sense of self-importance—our fleshly desire to make life about ourselves instead of God. When we find our identity in whom we know and with whom we're connected, it's the pride of life at work.

Satan tried to unravel the identity God had already established for Jesus, and he will do the same to us. He knows that if our primary identity is misaligned, we will do ministry for the wrong reasons. We will be driven by vanity. If our identity is not firmly established, every area of our lives will be affected. We will begin to manipulate people under us to make ourselves look, or feel, better. We will put up with abuse simply to be associated with "important" people.

But Satan's plan didn't work. Jesus' identity was in alignment, and He overcame temptation. He didn't have to turn stones into bread to know He had an identity as the Son of God. He said to the devil, "My identity does not come through what I do." Jesus didn't compromise His identity to acquire possessions. The devil said, "If you bow down, I'll give you everything your eyes can see." Jesus said, "My identity does not come through what I have." And Jesus did not give in to the pride of life. The devil said, "The angels will save you." Jesus said, "It's not about me."

If our identity is not established, it's easy to become tangled up in one, if not all three, of these webs. If we don't avoid these entanglements, our fortitude is at risk, as are the people we lead. This battle isn't easy. Many times, we're judged and celebrated for what people see externally. They can't see our internal motivations. Only God can see those.

When I was eleven or twelve, my Sunday school teacher was asked a question he could not answer. He was really stumped, and there was about 30 seconds of silence. The students stared at him. They couldn't believe it. This was the first time they'd seen him without an answer. I had the answer, only because it was something my mother had drilled into me. So I raised my hand, and all the kids stared at me instead. The teacher called on me, I gave the answer, the kids' jaws dropped, and the teacher said, "Good job, Wayne!" This happened three or four more times over the course of the year, and I became known as Wayne, the Bible Answer Man.

I'm going to be honest with you: it felt good to have the answers. It drove me to an unnatural place of study. One week they had another question that stumped the teacher and the class. Now, because this was my new identity, everybody looked at me for the answer. However, this time, despite all my studying and diligence, I did not have the answer. In that moment, something happened to me. Bible Answer Man had come up empty. If our identity is not in alignment, when our performance suffers, our sense of self-worth will suffer, too.

Early in ministry, I had difficulty separating my identity from my possessions. At first, I wasn't sure why I was struggling with this. Then my mind drifted back to elementary school. My stepfather, the primary breadwinner for the family, had lost his job as an aerospace engineer. Our lives took a drastic turn. We lost some of our possessions. We went from driving nice cars to driving my grandfather's '77 Cadillac—in the '90s. This bucket of a car dropped me off in front of my private school—a school at which I was the only African-American student. It was much more advanced than the public school I'd gone to previously, so I flunked that year. I tell you all this just so you'll know that this was the low point in my young life...until Grandparents' Day.

My grandparents were *regal*. If you've ever seen *Coming to America*, picture James Earl Jones, the King Jaffe Joffer, along with this wife, Aoleon. Minus the rose petals and the entourage, that was my grand-parents. My grandmother would wear an entire fox on her shoulder with a fur hat, and my grandfather would show up in his custom suit.

The entire class stopped when my grandparents stepped through the door in all their splendor. They said, "We're here to pick up Wayne." I'm telling you, I put my shoulders back, put my head up, and walked with pride all the way out of the school. They took me out to eat and then to get brand-new shoes. They didn't bargain shop either. My grandfather took me to Foot Locker and said, "Get whatever you want." Then, right before he brought me back to campus, he gave me fifty dollars!

The next day, I went to the grocery store and got change for that fifty. I told them to give me forty ones in a tin. I took that money and wrapped the tin around those forty ones so it looked like I had a pocketful of money. I went to school the next day and pulled my wad out to buy a snack, and all the kids crowded around me. They looked at my shoes and the money in my hand and said, "Man, you must be rich!" I remember that sense of failure fleeing. I remember the sense of worthlessness subsiding.

I went from being someone pushed to the periphery to being a primary figure in that school. It all surrounded a new pair of shoes and (what appeared to be) a pocketful of money. It was incremental, but that carried into my middle school years, my high school years, and even into early adulthood. What's interesting is that, while I was in ministry, God did a work in my heart. I loved him with all of my heart, but my identity was still tangled up in what I *had*. I was opposed to people truly interacting with me. As a result, others saw what I had before they actually saw me.

I could've written about many different areas of alignment, but this one is so foundational. If our identity is not well-established, we run the risk of abusing both ourselves and others in the place we're called to serve. We also run the risk of burning ourselves or others out in the long run.

So, be honest. Do you ever identify yourself according to what you have, or how *much* you have? Do you find your identity in the important, famous, or successful people you know? Do people know who you know before they know you? Do you identify yourself with your performance? Are you caught up in Lawrence's cycle of grief? I love the fact that Lawrence doesn't end his presentation with the cycle of grief, but with the cycle of grace.

The cycle of grace states that, first, we are accepted by God. Acceptance comes before we ever do anything for Him. Second, God is our sustenance. Our resources are constantly renewed through dependence on Him and Him alone. Out of that dependence, our identity is established. Our sense of significance does not come through our performance, possessions, or position, but through the fact that we are accepted and sustained by God. Finally, out of that place of well-established identity, we are able to offer our services to Him and to others, and achieve great things for His glory.

In closing, I have a request for you. No matter where you are in life—whether you've seen successes or failures this year; whether you have an abundance or a lack; whether your congregation is swelling to overflowing or you've got a gathering of just a few souls—please, take a moment to feel, to experience, and to rest in the love of the Father. Please allow yourself to feel the pleasure that God feels for you, His son or His daughter. If this most basic alignment is adjusted—if your identity is firmly established—then great works will come from that place of holiness.

chapter 5

THE FOUR WHEELS OF ALIGNMENT

JACIN HUMPHREY

GOD HAS TAKEN ME on an incredible journey over the last 15 years. I'm excited to share what I've learned with you, because I know it's going to challenge you to grow. As I've gone through this season, God has continually brought me to scriptures that reinforced what I was learning. This is exciting and encouraging to me. Any time you're going through a stretching phase and you see that same phase occurring in the Word, you know you're on the right track. You know God has you right where He wants you.

Years ago, I began to study for a bachelor's degree in music and business administration. I wanted to be in the business side of music. During an internship in Nashville,

I realized that if I was going to do anything in this field, I was going to have to move a lot. I decided that wasn't what I wanted to do with my life. I had big dreams, but I didn't know how to get to where I wanted to be. Thus began my season of trying to figure out what to do. I finished my MBA, got my first job in accounting and finance, and quickly learned that I didn't have the personality for that career. I did it for about four years and really disliked my life. I kept asking, "Why am I here? Where am I going?"

Then, I had an opportunity to jump into IT project management, and it was a Godsend. Within a short time, I was a certified project management professional and a full-time project manager. I began leading multimillion dollar projects that impacted the entire health care systems and the revenue streams of hospitals. The projects were typically managed by people with 15 or more years' experience, yet there I was with four or five years' experience, able to do it. I was engaged with everyone in my organization, from the cleaning crew all the way up to the C-level cabinet members.

I made one more stop before coming into full-time ministry two years ago. My last stop was at a worldwide business conglomerate that owned 60 companies across the globe. I was brought in to help build a project management office, to recruit and train project managers, and to implement software across the organization. My first project was installing a piece of software at 60 different companies across the globe. This was a huge project. Every company's installation was different. So my first task with my new company was to personally touch all 60 subsidiaries. I was only 34 years old.

It's not that I'm incredibly smart or politically savvy enough to maneuver myself into such opportunities. These positions were above my experience level. I jumped over some of my peers. And while I do like to think that I have some brains, what allowed me to see such rapid success in my life was my ability to come into alignment with how God does promotion. Because of how I handled myself during these years, I saw God's favor and blessing on my life—and I want the same favor and blessing on your life. I want to see God move you into promotion—not because of how you perform, but because of how you come into alignment with Him. Then *He* brings the promotion.

When you align yourself, you release your God-given potential and open your life up to promotion. So the question is, how do you align yourself? I like to think of a set of four tires: if the four wheels are out of alignment, you're going to shimmy and shake, and it's going to be difficult to reach your destination. But if the four wheels are in alignment, you're good to go!

THE FIRST WHEEL

The first wheel of alignment is to *align yourself.* What does this look like? To align yourself, you've got to know yourself. In any situation you're in, the most common denominator is *you*. What is your relationship with yourself like? How do you view yourself? What foundation are you working with?

You want success, and you want blessing; but if the Lord gave these things to you right now, what would happen? Would your life fall apart, like a house built on an unstable foundation? We see this happen so often with successful people: they have great hopes, ambition, and drive, but they achieve public success only to suffer private failures.

So, who are you? First of all, you are not what you do. Your identity is your *who*, not your *do*. Neither are you your childhood, experiences, hurts, or issues. So, if you're not any of these things, who are you really, at the deepest level? Who is the real you?

How do you define significance in your life? How do you define greatness? How do you settle the hurts of unforgiveness that keep you from connecting with others in a healthy way? Have you learned to handle your fear, your dreams, and the potential God has put on your life? How do you view these things, and your role in them? You've got to establish and understand your relationship with yourself in order to build a solid foundation.

Another aspect of aligning yourself is knowing your potential. You have significant potential inside of you, and you need to realize and remember that. Ephesians 2:10 says, "For we are God's handiwork, created in

Christ Jesus to do good works, which God prepared in advance for us to do."

God created you and put potential in you to do great things. John 15:8 says, "This is to my Father's glory, that you bear much fruit, showing yourselves to be my disciples." God wants you to bear fruit. He wants you to be productive. He wants you to do things. He has created you for this purpose. John 15:16 reads, "You did not choose me, but I chose you and appointed you so that you might go and bear fruit—fruit that will last." God wants you to tap into the potential that's inside of you; but first, you've got to know that it's there.

You have life-changing potential inside of you. You have the potential to change environments—to change the world. To come into alignment with God, you have to see yourself the way He sees you. You are a person who, when connected to God and aligned with His purpose, can do anything and everything He wants to do through you.

This is what we see in Philippians 4:13: "I can do all this through Him who gives me strength." God has put potential in your life, so come into alignment with Him and see yourself the way He sees you. See the potential He's put inside you!

THE SECOND WHEEL

You've aligned yourself. You know who you are. Now, you need to *align your dreams.* Before you can do this, you need to know what your dreams are. God has given each of us dreams and desires. Sometimes, we have these dreams and don't realize they're God-given. Your dreams are good and valuable because they came from God. Psalm 37:4 says, "Take delight in the Lord, and he will give you the desires of your heart." God knows the desires in your heart, because He put them there and wants to see them come to fruition! Proverbs 16:9 says, "In their hearts humans plan their course, but the Lord establishes their steps." God puts dreams inside of you, and He wants to bring those dreams to pass. He has a plan for you. We see this in Jeremiah 29:11: "'For I know the plans I have for you,' declares the Lord."

Now, you may be thinking, "You know, I had a dream once; but God didn't allow it to be fulfilled," Allow me to encourage you: don't confuse an outcome as an unmet dream expectation. God will often meet your desires in unexpected ways. Many times, we feel that a dream has been abandoned, only to look back later in life and realize that it has come to pass—just not in the way we'd planned.

This has happened to me. From the age of 16 until I was about 30, I played music with worship teams. My ultimate desire was to be a worship leader. When I was 16 or 17, God gave me a vision of me standing on stage, leading worship in front of thousands of people. I didn't know what to do with that dream. To be honest, it kind of scared me.

At the time, I was part of a huge church in Alabama. The first time I stepped foot on the stage, I looked out at an auditorium of 1,500 people. I looked into cameras streaming to almost 10,000 more. In that moment, I saw the same vision I had seen as a young man. God was showing me that, while I wasn't the one leading the worship, I was part of a team ushering thousands of people into God's presence through music. In that moment, God said, "See? This is the dream I put in you—the dream you thought you had to give up on because you weren't where you thought you needed to be. This is what I created you for."

Once you've aligned your dreams, you need to die to them. In other words, God wants you to be willing to trust *Him* to make those dreams come to pass. This is difficult. When God puts a dream in our hands, we often close our fists, hold onto it and say, "This is *my* dream, *my* promise, God." However, God gave you that dream to impact others, and He can't get it out of you if you've got it in a death grip. If we'll open our hands and allow God to get at that dream for *His* purposes, we'll position ourselves for promotion. Effectively, surrender says, "God, You've given me this dream, and I'm going to surrender it back to You. I don't know how it's going to happen, but I know You've given it to me, and I know you're faithful."

Jeremiah 10:23 says, "Lord, I know that people's lives are not their own; it is not for them to direct their steps." It's for God to direct your steps. Part of dying to your dreams is believing they will come to pass in His timing—believing He's in charge of the timetable. If He gave you the dream, it's His responsibility to make it come to pass. All we need to do is stay in alignment with Him and keep moving forward; He does the rest.

We find a great example of this principle in the life of Abraham. For many years, Abraham wanted a son. In his old age, he hadn't had one. Then, God gave him a promise: "I'm going to make you the father of many nations. Go out, Abraham, and look up at the stars. Count the stars, as many as you can count. That's how many your offspring will be." Then Abraham had Isaac. God said, "Abraham, I need you to go sacrifice Isaac. I need you to kill the one promise I gave you."

Abraham had to make a decision in that moment: "What do I do with the promise God has given me? Do I hold on to it, and say, 'No, God, you promised me I would have an heir!' Or do I open my fist and say, 'God, you gave this gift to me, so if I need to sacrifice Isaac, I'm going to do it. I have faith in the fact that you are still going to bring your promise to fruition'?" Abraham chose the second option. God's promise held firm. An angel appeared and told Abraham, "Stop! Go grab that ram and sacrifice it. God wanted to know if you were willing to die to your own dream."

THE THIRD WHEEL

Once you've aligned yourself and your dreams, you need to *align your vision*. This has been the hardest part of my journey: aligning my vision to my leader's vision. Our goal should be to further the vision of the one over us. Again and again in Scripture, God orchestrates the election of kings, principalities, rulers. God moves in the earth with ultimate authority; so we have to believe He's given our leaders the visions they have.

If we believe that, why do we try so often to pursue our own vision instead of following our leaders'? When we do this, we often end up with two (or more) visions. Multiple visions result in *division*. Choosing your own vision over your leader's will cause division on your team.

Psalm 133:1 says, "How good and pleasant it is when God's people live together in unity!" Unity with your leader, your team, and your family doesn't always equal agreement. Unity, rather, means a unified vision, where people choose to submit and stay humble. When division strikes, we often find ourselves in position paralysis: we can't move forward because we can't agree on where we're going.

If you're not championing your leader's vision, and you're stuck in position paralysis, you're merely taking up a seat. We're not called to fill roles for the sake of filling them. We're not called just to maintain the status quo. God calls and empowers us to move ministry *forward*, to move our families *forward*, and to move our organizations *forward*.

I'm not suggesting that you give up on your dreams or your calling. You still have those dreams; however, instead of pushing that agenda, you need to say, "God, I know You'll make my dreams happen. In the meantime, I'm going to serve the vision of the leader you've put over me."

Think of King David. Many, many years passed between the moment Samuel anointed him as King of Israel and the moment he actually became King of Israel. God gave him a promise at an early age. In the interim, he would be hunted by a vengeful king who wanted to kill him. When King Saul went into a cave to relieve himself, and David had a chance to kill him, David did *not forward his own agenda*. He chose to honor God and God's timing by not killing the king and fast-tracking himself to the throne. He said, "You know what, God? This is not my purpose to pursue. I will become the king as You promised, but I'm going to do it in Your timing. You are going to establish me as king. I am not going to establish myself as king."

Protect your leader's vision. Champion it, coach it, teach it, and train it—do whatever it takes to keep your leader's vision in front of the rest of your organization.

Another way to keep your vision aligned is to keep your *words* aligned. It's imperative that we watch our language—what we say about our visions, our bosses, and our peers. These words determine our effectiveness. Every word out of your mouth either promotes

God's purposes or plays into the hands of the enemy. Every word either advances God's calling on your life or sows seeds of discord, division, and disunity.

Let vision be the filter through which you view everything. Let your leader's vision be the filter through which you make decisions.

THE FOURTH WHEEL

Lastly, you need to *align your journey.* God is a God of the process, not only the destination. He wants to see how we handle ourselves along the way more than He wants to see us cross the finish line. For this reason, it's important to travel your journey with grace—grace for your leaders, your peers, and yourself.

What does this mean on a daily basis? It means trusting our leaders, even when we don't agree with them. Remember, God is leading them. Jeremiah 17:7 says, "But blessed is the one who trusts in the Lord, whose confidence is in him." You'll be blessed if you put your confidence in the Lord and how He orchestrates lives. Proverbs 16:3 reads, "Commit to the Lord whatever you do, and He will establish your plans." Instead of pushing your own agenda, be a helper. Step back and say, "God, I just want to help. How do I help in this situation to forward *Your vision* and *Your agenda* for this organization?"

Additionally, forget about your own timing. I see older people fall into this trap, because they feel that their time is limited. They may think, *I've got a calling on my life, but I've only got a few years left to walk in it. I've got to do it now!* Let me encourage you with Joel 2:25: "I will repay you for the years the locusts have eaten." What does this Scripture tell us? The Lord can do more through a few submitted years, a few *aligned* years, than He can with many selfish years. Don't worry about the time you have left. In fact, surrender your timing to the Lord, and accept His timing!

Another part of aligning your journey is building relationships and leveraging influence. Everyone has a filter through which they see the world: this includes your leader, your peers, your family, your spouse, and your children. A filter determines how someone interprets information. Our filters are shaped by life experiences and family dynamics. Take time to build relationships with people so that you understand their filters. If you understand how they see things, you can understand how to effectively communicate with them; and this will prevent a lot of frustration along your journey.

In my life, I've created job security and promotional potential for myself by taking it upon myself to make my leader's life easier. What would it look like if we all took on the role of a servant? What if everyone worked to make their leaders' lives easier? What if leaders worked to serve those they lead?

Another way to align your journey is to fuel the health of your team. Your team has to be healthy to be effective, and you have a role in contributing to that health. If you don't, you contribute to its decline. We need to hold one another accountable to the vision. We need to lead our teams into maturity. Help your teammates have the hard conversations. Help them stay healthy by making sure they have clear expectations.

My final advice for aligning your journey? Get to work. Really go after it, and crush it. Watch God promote His agenda through you, and promote you in the process.

Imagine two fields. You are the farmer, and you have a field to plow. You can easily get distracted by your neighbor's field because it's bigger and produces more fruit; but then what happens? You'll slow down or stop plowing your own field. Increase the field that God has given you to plow—whatever it may be! Plow the field you're given until God gives you a different one. Think of Elijah and Elisha. When Elijah found Elisha, what was he doing? He was *plowing his own field*. He was hard at work, serving where God had placed him. Then Elijah came along and said, "The Lord has something great for you. In fact, you're going to do even more than I have done." Because Elisha was working hard at the task God had given him, God brought promotion into his life.

These are four simple, yet difficult, areas of alignment that will bring significant favor and blessings into your life. May God give you peace as you develop leadership skills, an understanding of His perspective of you, and the courage to do the hard work. May He give you dreams and allow you to serve others as you wait on His timing for those dreams. May He give you passion to support the vision you're under, and the bravery to lead if that's what's needed. May God give you the maturity and the grace to walk your journey well.

chapter 6

ALIGNMENT ACROSS GENERATIONS

SAM CHAND

'M A LEADERSHIP CONSULTANT in my mid-60s, and I work with people from multiple generations. Some are older than me, but most are younger. I have learned from experience that generational alignment within an organization (as well as among multiple cooperating organizations) is the key to progress.

When I go into an organization, I do four things: assess, articulate, align, and help advance. First, I assess the situation: what does this organization want to do? What's their vision? What's their vehicle? I use these insights to articulate a plan that will move them forward. Then, I work to bring the organization—people, resources, systems, and structures—into alignment.

Last, I help advance them to what's next. Assess, articulate, align, and advance. I do those four things—always in that order. Do you want to know which one is always the hardest?

That's right: alignment. This is where the heavy lifting comes in. Until this point, it's all just talk. Trying to pull everything, and everyone, together in the same direction is hard work, especially when you have people from multiple generations at the table. Alignment is so crucial. Think about how you align yourself with the weather. If it's cold outside, you need to wear a coat, scarf, hat, and gloves, or you'll freeze. If it's hot and humid, you do *not* wear a coat, scarf, hat, and gloves. Here's another example: think of your eyes' alignment—how they move, blink, cry, and see in tandem with one another. If one eye does its own thing, you're in trouble. Likewise, in a recipe, all the ingredients and utensils work together in just the right way to create something scrumptious. If even one gets out of alignment—say, the salt—you have a bad dish.

If you want to make a purchase, your finances must be in alignment. If you make a decision, how you communicate it better be in alignment with the decision itself. If you have a vision, you need programming aligned with that vision, or you'll send the wrong signals. No matter what the arena—business, church, ministry, family, organization—alignment is necessary. With this in mind, think about the multiple generations involved in different areas of your life. Did you know that there are six generations alive in the US today who attend your church and work with you? Let me break these groups down for you (population numbers as of 2015):

- The G.I. Generation, born 1901-1926: 2 million people.
- The Mature Generation, or "Silents," born 1927-1945. 30 million people.
- The Baby Boomers, born 1946-1964. 83 million people.
- Generation X, born 1965-1980. You don't hear much about them, but they are strong: 66 million people.
- The Millennials, or Generation Y, born 1981-2000: 83 million people (fifty percent of Millennials are parents, so don't think of them as kids).
- Generation Z—we call them the "Boomlets," born after 2001. They began graduating from high school in 2018: 73 million people.

Each of these generations was raised by the two before it. Millennials were raised by Boomers and X-ers. Gen Z-ers were raised by X-ers and Millennials. All of these groups compete with and push against one another. For example, almost 40 percent of US workers have a boss who is younger than they are. This can clearly create challenges. We have workers who are thinking, "I've been here and done this for years. Who are you? You don't know anything. I've got children older than you!"

I'm almost 65. My two Millennial daughters run all of my businesses, which results in interesting conversations. We're coming at things from two different worldviews. I'm coming from a stabilized point of view, and they're coming from a view that says, "Hey! Let's go after this!" Their risk threshold is different. I take things more personally than they do, and they can absorb or shake things off more easily than I can. They even measure quality of life differently than I do. It's important to them to balance family time, hanging out with friends, and taking vacations. The generational variety in my life and businesses creates quite a dynamic atmosphere!

However, this doesn't mean we should create an "us vs. them" mentality. Let's discard that notion right up front. My empirical data supports the fact that age doesn't determine how someone thinks. I know 25-year-olds who are old in their thinking, and I know 87-year-olds who are young in theirs. We can't lump people together according to their generations and make assumptions: "Well, they're Millennials, so we treat them all like a monolithic group of people." No, that doesn't work.

Let's consider two important words, and then we'll look at how Jesus handled the trans-generational challenge. The two words are observations and opinions. Every one of us observes things, and we all form opinions—quickly, I might add. We look at someone and instantly think, "I don't like her." Reflect on how you behave with a remote control in your hand. How long does it take you to change the channel? You observe what's on the screen, form an opinion (sometimes in less than a second), and think, "I don't want to watch that." You press the button. A similar thing happens when you walk into a restaurant. You look around, observe, and form an opinion about the restaurant based on what you see, smell, and hear.

This is what I've found: every one of us is a product of somebody else's observations and opinions. Pastor Van Moody observed me, formed an opinion of me, and invited me to be a part of this book project. I get to write this for you because he observed me and formed an opinion. His opinion was, "I am willing to take a risk with this guy, and let people read what he has to say." Everything is about opinions, which are formed from observations.

Someone only gets a promotion because a supervisor observed her and formed a good opinion. Someone only gets fired because a supervisor observed him and formed a bad opinion. Two people only get married because they've observed each other and formed opinions. These two actions go together, and everyone performs them. We have become a product of this process.

Every person in this world is doing what they're doing because somebody observed and formed an opinion about them.

So what does all this have to do with alignment, or multigenerational leadership?

We are all forming opinions, but here's the downside: if our opinions aren't favorable, we keep people down. We hold them back. It may not be their fault. They may not deserve to be held back, but our opinions do this anyway.

Our opinions matter. Let's look at Luke 2:46-47:

After three days they found Him in the temple courts, sitting among the teachers, listening to them and asking them questions. Everyone who heard Him was amazed at His understanding and His answers.

Jesus was twelve years old in these verses. Every year, His parents joined the caravan to Jerusalem. They would arrive, have a grand time worshipping, and then leave to go home. But this year, after three days of homeward travel, Mary and Joseph realized Jesus wasn't with them. They'd probably thought He was with relatives, but He wasn't, and panic set in. They returned to Jerusalem and began looking for Jesus. This was no easy task. Jerusalem wasn't a small place. It was a labyrinth of alleyways, streets, and cobblestones.

When they found Jesus, He was sitting among the scholars. How did He get there? We don't know how He behaved or what He did; but whatever it was He did, those men made observations and formed opinions that led them to allow Jesus to sit with them. That's a significant accomplishment for a twelve-year-old!

Jesus' parents found him doing four things. The first thing is that they find Him *hearing*. Jesus was listening to the scholars. The second thing it says is that He was *asking them questions*. Third, He *understood*; and last, we see that He was *giving answers*.

I was born and raised in India, in a culture not all that different from the one Jesus lived in. In the culture in which I grew up, unless you were over 40, you really didn't have anything to say. When Paul wrote to Timothy, "Let no man despise your youth," he wasn't writing to a child. He was talking to an adult, but one younger than those he taught. So the question for us is, how does a twelve-year-old in a patriarchal society arrest the attention of learned, older people? These were rabbis—Sadducees and Pharisees—the scholars of that time. Jesus was allowed to sit down with them. How did this kid speak to the older generation? How did he affect their observations and opinions? How does this happen?

Try to picture the temple: its pillars, its dust, the kids playing everywhere. Then, picture a twelve-year-old hanging around these older men and just listening in. Suddenly, His squeaky voice piped up with a question. And, while we so often lead a conversation with answers, notice that this isn't what Jesus did. He started by listening to them. Here's what I want to say to all generations: please, *please* learn the great art of active listening. When you listen, you hear things you would otherwise miss.

After Jesus heard them, He asked a question *so* He could gain understanding. He wasn't asking a question simply to give a response, nor was He trying to set them up to look stupid. Has anyone ever asked you a question in order to set you up? It's not a pleasant experience. Often, it doesn't matter what answer you give, because they've come prepared with a statement. Of course, this was not Jesus' motivation. By sitting down, He became part of them. Then, He listened and asked questions so He could gain understanding and speak answers into their lives. We can follow this example. We can sit down with people, actively listen, ask probing questions, work to understand, and then speak into their lives. It is this type of alignment that will get you invited to sit in the circle again.

We find multigenerational alignment by following Jesus' example. But finding it is not enough. We need to maintain alignment. And when things get out of alignment, we need to make corrections. Misaligned people are not self-correcting. When my car is out of alignment, I take it to the garage and they jack it up. Sometimes, people require similar treatment. We're tempted to take a tolerant attitude to misaligned people—to simply wait, hoping they will align themselves.

This does not happen. I've never found out-of-alignment people who align themselves. It always takes an external force—another voice or perspective—to bring alignment.

Once we've found alignment, we must guard it tenaciously so things don't go out of alignment again. You've got to fight for it. When a team member is going out of alignment, you've got to bring them back. Pay attention to the words they use, which may alert you to a change in perspective. Pay attention if someone seems depressed. You've got to address these struggles so that your group can stay in alignment.

You may ask, "Which comes first: organizational alignment or personal alignment? Do people align before a company aligns? Do members align before churches align?" I can tell you that, when people align, organizational alignment takes place much more easily.

I want to conclude by listing a few things that everyone wants—universal desires. This isn't just what Millennials want, or Z-ers, or Boomers. *Everyone* wants these things. Not a single person can read this list and say, "I don't want that." Here's the list:

Honor and respect. Honor is about the person, while respect is about the performance. You may honor people without respecting them, and you may respect a person without honoring them. Everybody craves both honor *and* respect.

A safe environment. Everybody desires safety: physically, emotionally, psychologically, and relationally.

Growth. You need to create a learning organization, where everybody knows they are expected, allowed, and encouraged to learn, mature, and get further down the road than they were when they started.

Fun. I hate it when you encounter places so focused on their work that they never have fun. Fun is the glue that keeps people together! Fun helps people to create relationships. Make sure you're making space for it.

Authentic relationships. People want to be coached, befriended, and encouraged by others. This gives them a sense of belonging.

Self-worth and a sense of accomplishment. Everybody wants to leave their workplace each day saying, "That was worth it! I made a difference."

Dialogue. People aren't robots. They want dialogue with other humans. Someone might say, "Don't just bark at me. Don't yell at me. Talk to me as if I matter. I know you could say it in a sentence, but say it in a paragraph."

Clarity of vision. People need to know what they're working for and toward. Without this end goal in mind, they're simply doing meaningless busywork.

Leadership. People need clear direction. They need someone to follow.

It doesn't matter what age bracket you're in or what generation you're from—you want these things, and the people you lead want these things. Having them in your organization will help you have multigenerational alignment.

Let me share one more story with you. Many people were moving to the city of Rome. There were so many Jews that the Roman citizens became concerned: "There are more of them than us!" So, the Roman leaders went to the Pope and said, "Your Holiness, there are too many Jews here! We've got to get them out of this city, or they're going to take over. We want you to kick them out!"

The Pope said, "No, they're good people. They're fine people. They're helping us."

But the Romans were so belligerent and aggressive about the whole thing that the Pope finally acquiesced and decreed that all Jews had to leave Rome in three days.

When the Jews found out they had to leave town, they were upset. They went to the Pope and said, "Your Holiness, how can you do this to us? We're good people—good citizens. We contribute to the economy and the workforce."

The Pope said, "Well, that's how it is."

The Jews said to the Pope, "We would like to give you a challenge. On a certain day in St. Peter's Square, let's have a theological debate. If we win, we get to stay. If we lose, you can kick us out."

The Pope said, "Sure."

The Jews said, "Oh, except for one thing. This debate will be with no talking. Nobody will talk."

The Pope said, "Sure. I'm the theologian. No problem."

So the Jews went looking for somebody who would debate for them. At first, they couldn't find anyone willing to go up against the Pope. Then, they found an uneducated street sweeper named Moishe who was willing.

On the big day, there was a large platform in St. Peter's Square. The Pope was on one side with the cardinals. Moishe the street sweeper stood on the other side, surrounded by rabbis. The debate began.

The Pope twirled his index finger above his head.

Moishe pointed his index finger downward.

The Pope held up three fingers.

Moishe wagged one finger at him.

The Pope pulled out the Lord's Supper, communion, and began to partake.

Moishe pulled out an apple and started munching it.

All of a sudden, the Pope stood up and said, "He's too good! The Jews can stay!" Then he left, flustered. The Jews were jubilant. The cardinals crowded around the Pope asking, "Your Holiness, what happened?"

The Pope answered, "When I said to him, 'God is all around us,' he said, 'God is right here as well.' When I said, 'I believe in God the Father, God the Son, and God the Holy Spirit,' he said, 'But don't we all believe in the same Father?' And when I pulled out the Lord's Supper to remind him of the sanctification and the cleansing that comes from communion, he pulled out the apple to remind me how it all started!"

On the other side, the rabbis surrounded Moishe asking, "What happened?"

Moishe answered, "Well, when he said, 'I'm going to clear Rome of all you Jews,' I said, 'We're staying right here.' When he said, 'You've got three days to leave,' I said, 'Not one of us is leaving.'" They asked him what had happened at the end. He said, "Oh, well, he pulled out his lunch, so I pulled out mine."

And that is how life is. We go through life giving signals—through our words, our writings, our work, our art, and our body language. What you try to communicate often isn't heard because of a lack of alignment.

But if we're going to accomplish anything, we need to have effective communication. We need to be in alignment. You need to be in alignment with God, your church, your business, your family, your neighbors, your friends, those you lead, and those who lead you—because when you are aligned, everything works out for you.

chapter 7

HOW'S YOUR VERTICAL ALIGNMENT?

KENNETH ULMER

A S WE LEAD, positioning ourselves with God and His people, we must be mindful of alignment. Most of the time, we think of alignment as a linear concept; but it is more than that. When I was in the Marine Corps, to be in alignment, you had to be in line behind the person in front of you, as well as aligned with those on either side of you. Alignment, for us, was three-dimensional. In leadership, I want to add a fourth direction.

As leaders, whom you are lined up behind is not the most important thing. Neither is the person you're lined up with on either side. The most important alignment for leaders is the vertical one. By that, I mean that we live and lead God's people by being aligned with the will and Word of God.

We see this principle in action with Moses. Look at Exodus 33:12-13:

Moses said to the Lord, "You have been telling me, 'Lead these people,' but you have not let me know whom you will send with me. You have said, 'I know you by name and you have found favor with me.' If you are pleased with me, teach me your ways so I may know you and continue to find favor with you."

Moses asks God for the ability to lead His people. Moses was a great leader—one of the greatest in biblical history. He leads a nation out of Egyptian captivity and toward the Promised Land. In the midst of this journey, Moses stops and prays a profound prayer. He essentially says, "Lord, my heart's desire is to know you." Even as a great leader, his ultimate priority in life is to know God. He's asking, "God, reveal your ways to me so that I may know You."

It's interesting to me that, by the time Moses prays this prayer, he already knows God's name. Remember when Moses first encounters God in the burning bush? God says, "I want you to take the message to the people."

Moses, knowing his own name holds no power, replies, "When they ask me who sent me, what name do I give them?"

God answers, "Tell them, 'I AM has sent me to you.'"

So way back then, Moses learned God's name, but here he is, thirty chapters later, wanting to know God relationally. He did not yet know God on the level that his heart desired to know Him.

As leaders, we teach people *about* God. We tell them His name. We describe who He is. Week in and week out, we stand in front of people and want them to know *about* God. Notice that this is not Moses' prayer. He doesn't ask to know *about* God. He asks to *know Him*—personally, intimately, in a very real way.

How many of us stand at the pulpit before the people of God and share our knowledge *about* God? How many of us share from our relationship with God? Do we know him relationally, personally, intimately? If we do, are we sharing what we've gleaned from that relationship? Ask yourself, "Am I ministering, preaching, and teaching out of my knowledge *about* God, or out of my relationship *with* God?" We learn from Moses that the most significant priority of a leader is to know God personally.

Let's take a closer look at Moses' prayer. In it, he reveals the process for knowing God: "Show me your ways so I can know you." Before Moses can know God, he has to learn His ways. Knowing the ways of God is the path to knowing Him personally. If God reveals to me His methodology—how He flows, how He operates, and how He interacts with me and others—I will know Him personally.

This path, this process, never ends. We must continuously seek to learn His ways so that we continue to be in relationship with Him. In Isaiah 55:8, God says, "For My thoughts are not your thoughts, neither are your ways My ways." We can desire to know His ways every moment of every day; but we're still never going to learn them all. Our faith road is a never-ending discovery process. God says (I paraphrase), "If you want to know how different our ways are, look at the heavens. As high as they are, that's how much higher My thoughts are than yours!" But God doesn't say this to deter us from learning His ways. He doesn't tell us not to try. He simply wants to show us how much there is to learn.

Hence, when we can't quite understand some of His ways, we must lean on faith. As Hebrews 11:1 says, "Now faith is confidence in what we hope for and assurance about what we do not see." To know God personally, we must know Him through personal experience. But, to know God personally, we must also know Him through faith, because we're trying to comprehend the incomprehensible; we're trying to see the invisible and know the unknowable. God hasn't yet fully made himself known to us; still, He desires to be known. So we seek to know him, through both interaction and faith, and we lead others out of this personal relationship with Him—out of the lessons we've learned along the path of seeking His ways.

Let's take a closer look at this verse from Isaiah. God says, "My thoughts are not your thoughts." "Thoughts" is a picture word. It depicts a process of interpenetrating, blending, bringing together, plaiting, or braiding. God plaits, or braids, together different elements of our lives to bring us into the revelation of who He is. How does God think? What are His ways? He brings together the various elements of our lives—the good and bad, the ups and downs, the right and wrong, the sunshine and the rain. When He weaves them together, they become the revelation of God's will for our lives. He always operates in a manner that brings glory to Himself.

In Exodus 33:13, Moses speaks to God. The NASB translates his prayer this way: "If I have found favor in Your sight, let me know Your ways that I may know You, so that I may find favor in Your sight." Moses understands how this works. God gives him favor, and as a result, Moses can learn His ways. By working to know God's ways, Moses is granted favor. It's a beautiful, continuous cycle: Have God's favor; seek God's ways; have God's favor.

There is an anointing on your life. There is a call of God on your life. There is favor over your life. There is favor over your ministry, your marriage, and your gifts. God has laid His hands on you. Don't take that lightly! It's not because of how smart or attractive you are. It's not because of your degrees or the letters after your name. It's the favor of God. There are people more talented than you who have not accomplished what you've accomplished, and there are people less talented than you who have accomplished much more. This isn't a simple case of cause and effect; this is the favor of God at work! And if you want to continue to live and walk in that favor, you must guard and defend it.

How do we protect that favor? We must continually work to understand how God works, how He operates, and how He moves. As we seek this understanding, we walk so closely with God that He continues to grant us favor, and it never wavers. The NIV translates Exodus 33:13, "...so I may know you and continue to find favor with you." Finding favor is a continuous process that, if protected intentionally by seeking God's ways, need not be interrupted. We don't want to do anything to block His favor. We want to stay in it, to live in it, to minister in it. Father, don't let me lose this favor. Don't let me lose, damage, or disgrace this anointing.

Moses wanted to understand the dynamics of knowing God, and so should we. What does this look like? What happens when we know Him? The better we know God, the more our lives will be impacted, both spiritually and psychologically. How does knowing God impact me spiritually? If I don't know Him, my steps won't be aligned with His mind, ways, and will. But if I do know God's ways, I can ensure that, to the best of my limited ability, my prayers and goals are aligned with His will.

Slowly but surely, my entire life will become more adjusted to God's ways, His methods, and His plans. I pray, "Not my will, but *Thy* will," and I behave according to this prayer, this sincere desire. The more I seek to know and understand God's ways, the more His desires become my own.

Learning about God's ways also impacts me psychologically. When I was in sixth grade, God revealed Himself to me through Psalm 121:4: "Indeed, He who watches over Israel will neither slumber nor sleep. I learned something about God's ways, about how He operates: Whatever He's doing, He's doing it 24/7. God never sleeps. That means that I can go to bed. I can relax and rest. Psychologically, I can operate in a place of peace and contentment. I don't get caught up in the anxieties, the worries, the hustle and bustle. I don't get too far off to the left or the right, because, ultimately, I know God is on the case, no matter what time it is. What are God's ways? God's ways are around the clock.

Paul wrote, "Be anxious for nothing" (Philippians 4:6). Instead of worrying, pray about it, in alignment with God's will and ways as He's revealed them to you. Then you'll have the peace only God can give. Knowing the ways of God profoundly impacts me psychologically, because I adjust my prayers to His ways, and receive a sense of peace.

Now that we understand the tremendous impact of God's ways on and in our lives, let's look at the components of His ways. God's will is made up of three ingredients: His purpose, His preference, and His plan.

Let's look at purpose first. God's ways will always be in line with His purpose. And God's purpose for your life, ministry, marriage, family, teaching, preaching, business, and gifts is always that He may be honored and glorified. Everything He does will be aligned with this purpose. Speaking of purpose, everything has a purpose. You have a purpose in reading this. I have a purpose in writing it. The ultimate purpose of everyone, and everything, is to glorify God.

The second component of God's ways is His preference, which is revealed through His Word. The answer to, "How does God desire that we live?" is always the same: "It's in His Word." Where are the guidelines for living? In the Word. Does God prefer I live this way or that way? It's in the Word. If we're truly seeking to know and understand God's ways, we *must* live in alignment with God's preferences as revealed through the Bible. We must live under the authority of Scripture. We must live our lives following and walking in his Word.

It's not God's will that any should perish. How do we know this? It's in His Word. It's not God's will that you be defeated, or that any weapon be formed against you. How do we know this? His Word tells us so. God's preference is for you to walk in victory! His preferences are revealed through Scripture and are always in alignment with His will.

The final component of God's ways is His plan. Now, I'm going to tell you something pretty radical: *God's plan is always related to your will.* Sounds a little crazy, right? Stick with me. His *purpose* is always related to *His* will; His *preference* is always related to *His* will; but His *plan* is always related to *your will.* How? The revelation of God's will is not a cancellation of yours. When God reveals Himself through His Word, it doesn't cancel your ability to choose. He created you with the ability to make a choice, and it's up to you to choose whether to follow His will or not.

It always amazes me that God loves us enough to give us the ability to *not* love Him. He does not force you to love him, and I don't think you want God to force you. We make choices, and each choice comes with consequences. They're a package deal. We don't always know the consequences of a choice, but by making it, we choose the results nonetheless. When we choose to operate contrary to God's will, we choose the consequences that come along with that.

You may be in a situation right now in which you made a bad choice. Perhaps you're struggling with a crisis because you didn't trust God, and so you chose not to do things His way. Or maybe someone you love is in such a situation. Many people are dealing with unpleasant circumstances in their churches, marriages, homes, or finances because of choices they've made.

But not all is lost! Here's what I love about God: *God's purpose always trumps your plan.* God's plan will always be affected by yours, but that's never the end of the story. God's purpose overrules the circumstances you create. When you make a conscious, deliberate decision *not* to follow God's will, God is not done with you. He doesn't just kick you to the curb. He doesn't write you off. Praise God!

God's purpose is fixed, but His plan is flexible. His purpose for your life is to receive glory and honor, and that never changes. His plan is related to the choices you make. He loves you too much to leave you stranded at the end of your bad choices. His plan for you is still in effect.

Isaiah writes, "All we like sheep have gone astray" (53:6). Sheep are not the smartest animals. They don't just jump off the path. When sheep find food, they drop their heads and nibble the grass. Did you catch that? They drop their heads. They take their focus off the shepherd and focus on food. By the time they raise their heads, they're *way* off the path. God compares us to sheep because we, too, take our eyes off the Shepherd, put our gaze on our own plans, and go astray. Some of us turn away in a moment—in a blink. For others of us, it's not so sudden. Some of us turn slowly, one nibble at a time. We compromise this and that, until one day we look up and we're far, far away from where we're meant to be.

What have you been nibbling on? What is demonically, but systematically, drawing you away from the will of God? In what areas are you compromising? What principles are you bending? What boundaries are you stepping over (or flirting with)? No matter how you answer these questions, God's purpose trumps your plan, because He doesn't leave His sheep out to wander alone. The Good Shepherd goes after and finds His sheep, and then shifts His plan for them.

I love that God gives us the Holy Spirit, who doesn't let us stay comfortable when we wander. The Spirit of God remains in you even when you're astray, and He won't let you be satisfied. He won't let you settle down out there. If He has to, he'll whoop your behind and bring you back to where you should've stayed in the first place. Nevertheless, He'll adjust His plan, even when He has to chastise you. He loves you enough to take you from Plan A, which was to bless you, to Plan B, which is to do whatever it takes to bring you back into the fold and bless you anyway. All this is so that He will get the glory He is due.

Moses' prayer went something like this: "Lord, I want to know You. I want to know You intimately, personally, and relationally. I want to walk in the lifelong process of knowing You. I want to know You so that I guard the favor on my life. The way that I know You is through Your revelation of Your ways. I know that, ultimately, I can't get there completely; but I want to get closer. Lord, I want more of you. I want to grow closer to you every moment." There's no reason we can't pray this same prayer every day.

You are a leader in the Kingdom of God! God trusts you enough to put you in front of the people in your class, small group, or church. He's entrusted these people to you so that you can touch them for His sake, His honor, and His glory! Touch them out of the personal relationship that you have with God—a relationship you work on every day, to know Him intimately and guard His favor over your life and leadership.

Moses said, "Lord, I can't lead these people by myself. I can't do this by myself. Show me Your ways that I may know You—so my life is aligned with Your will, Your way, and Your Word."

chapter 8

HOW TO MAKE YOUR VISION A REALITY

SHAWN LOVEJOY

EVERY ORGANIZATION BEGINS with a vision; however, few finish with one. The question is, how do we get the vision statement on the wall to continue happening down the halls? The answer is alignment. Everyone involved with your vision must be aligned with it. How do we get everyone giving the vision life and breath? A vision statement is only as strong as the leader, because it's the leader who gives it life.

God tells us in Proverbs 29:18, "Where there is no vision, the people perish" (KJV). Where there is no vision, things die: organizations, groups, ministries, and churches. Where there is no vision, people die: leaders, volunteers, staff members, and CEOs. The corollary is also true. Where there *is* vision, there is energy, life, and a magnetism that attracts people.

Vision drives everything. You may have heard that culture eats vision for breakfast; however, vision is actually a foundational component of the culture you're trying to set. The first thing you need to do is get everyone to buy into the vision. Then, over time, you can project it.

We'll get into how to do all of this. First, let me share a little about myself. I'm a founder and CEO of a coaching ministry. Primarily, I am a husband and a father to three teenagers. They're all doing well right now, but let's be honest: it's volatile. I've taught the oldest to drive, and she's at college, standing on her own two feet and doing well. I've got two more to teach to drive. As a father, this scares me to death.

You know the drill: before you let your kid drive away from the house, you sit down and have a talk about the dos and don'ts. During these talks, I warn my children about a potential driving dilemma: hitchhikers. I tell my kids, "Avoid hitchhikers and don't pick them up."

Now, this may sound like the antithesis of the Christian life. After all, shouldn't we help people who are stranded and broken down? Isn't that what Jesus did? We who watch the news know the truth: hitchhikers can become hijackers. Once they're in the vehicle, they seize control and drive it far from the intended destination. Those inside the vehicle are susceptible to great harm and peril.

I've seen this happen in organizations hundreds of times—both nonprofits and churches. In fact, there's hardly a church plant I've encountered that didn't suffer an attempted coup in its first three years at the hands of people who went from vision-hitchhikers to vision-hijackers. These people seized control of the vision, either knowingly or unknowingly, and drove it miles off course, putting everyone involved in peril.

This is the primary reason that few churches finish with a vision—it gets hijacked. Through our coaching at Courage to Lead, hundreds of leaders have shared that this is one of the principle tensions they face. We teach on this topic, and I've written a book that is the culmination of my coaching on this issue. We call it "being mean about the vision." The word "mean" has multiple meanings. The first one that usually springs to mind is "unkind; cruel." However, the one we use most is "to have in mind as your purpose, to intend." We say, "I mean that as a compliment" or "What I mean to say..."

So when I say, "Be mean about the vision," I'm saying, "Be intentional." I'm not giving you permission to be a cruel pastor; though of course, I have known some mean pastors. To be mean about the vision means to be intentional with it. Be clear about it. Work to align everyone to it. Protect it.

I was a senior pastor for almost 17 years, and I'm most proud of three things: first, that we stayed true to our vision; second, that my wife liked me; and third, that my kids loved the church. Those are the most fulfilling things to me personally, and they will be to you, as well.

Therefore, I'd like to unpack eight ways you can keep your vision from getting hijacked.

STRATEGY 1: MAKE SURE YOUR VISION IS FROM GOD.

Everything has to start here. We can't skip this step. We need to make sure, with great clarity and certainty, that our vision is from God. The KJV translates Proverbs 29:18 this way: "Where there is no vision, the people perish." The NIV says, "Where there is no revelation, people cast off restraint." Both translations are true. The *vision* must be a *revelation* from God. We don't have to discover or invent it; God gives it to us. We are simply called to receive it and communicate it.

So, before we go running off to change the world, trying to tackle hell with a squirt gun, we need to be sure that our vision came from God. As a senior leader, I often correct my team members when they say, "Shawn's vision is..." I've never believed it's my vision; I know the vision for my organization is something that's been revealed to me by God.

Why is it important that I know this? For two reasons. First, because knowing the vision is from God gives me confidence to boldly communicate and protect it. Ask yourself, "Do I really believe my vision is from God? Is this my vision or His?" Second, it's important that we answer this because when we know our vision is from God, we'll be more likely to stay in the game when it's challenged, or when pursuing it becomes difficult. If it's merely our vision, we're more likely to give up when the going gets tough.

STRATEGY 2: KEEP THE VISION FROM LEAKING.

I think it was Bill Hybels, senior leader of Willow Creek Church, from whom I first heard the phrase "vision leaks." To protect your vision from being hijacked, you must keep it from leaking. Remember when we were kids, and birthday balloons were all made of latex instead of Mylar? We would try to take home as many as possible, because having a bunch of balloons made us feel so successful! We'd carry them home, thinking we'd keep them forever, and we'd fall asleep with them clinging to our ceiling. When we woke in the morning, what did we find? All the balloons on the floor. Slowly but surely, the energy in those balloons leaked out, and they lost their impact on us.

The same thing can happen in our organizations. If I may be so bold, I believe that vision leaks most quickly in leaders. Think about it: we're busy, we're going after it, we're manic, we're managing it...Sunday is always coming in the ministry world, just as Monday is always coming in the corporate world. We're under deadlines every day. Over time, we forget why we're doing it all. The most important thing we can do as leaders is to remember why we're here.

Let's be honest. Ninety-five percent of what we do is not sensational. It's checking our inbox. It's Google Drive. It's meetings. It's people—people who *drain* us. And over time, we lose our passion, we get discouraged and sometimes, we even want to quit. So if *we* forget why we're doing it all, how much more will this loss of vision begin to permeate our entire organizations?

One of the biggest lies from hell that I've ever believed as a pastor was that, if I could just get people to assimilate, we would close the back door. The truth is that people will go right out the back door if you're not constantly reminding them why they're with you. It's not sensational to park cars or hand out worship guides, or—heaven forbid—sit on the floor with a two-year-old who doesn't like to be told "No." These are difficult experiences that become far more so if people are not reminded why their jobs are so important.

As leaders, we have to consistently communicate the vision. We've got to tell success stories—remind people why we do what we do. Training is important, but the "why" is even more essential! In fact, when people understand the "why," they'll go above and beyond their job descriptions, because human beings are driven by "why," not "what."

How do we keep our vision from leaking? We have to daily reconnect with the Source of living water: we've got to spend time with God. When we know His vision for our lives, we can talk about it constantly. We don't cast visions so we can preach; we preach so we can cast vision. Everything flows around the vision. We don't decide what we're going to do next—the vision decides that. Rally people around the vision and celebrate it consistently. Remind people why they're with you. Continually call them back to what's important.

STRATEGY 3: CONFRONT VISION DRIFT QUICKLY.

Sometimes, people in our organization do things that make us wonder, "Do they really get it? Are they 100 percent on board?" We need to pay attention to these red flags. The Holy Spirit is trying to get your attention, in order for you to become a better leader. I see too many leaders who are cowardly, and will not involve themselves in courageous conversations. But this is what it takes to confront vision drift.

I'm not suggesting you accuse anyone without a reason; I'm suggesting that, with humility, you say, "Hey, it could just be me...but by your body posture, your passive-aggressive comments, your sarcasm, your lack of commitment, and the way you've been speaking out (or not speaking out) in meetings, I believe there could be some vision drift between the two of us. It could just be me, but I would be remiss not to talk to you about it." We need to make room for honesty. When we sense something isn't right, we need to confront it quickly. Clarity and accountability are both essential for your vision to become reality, and they're necessary to aligning everyone in the organization.

STRATEGY 4: RECOGNIZE THAT ALL PROGRAMMING AND STRUCTURE IS PART OF THE VISION.

Let me confess something else; I think this will encourage you. In all my years as a senior leader, I've never had anyone walk up to me and say, "I'm not on board with the vision." I *have* had people sit in my office or stand in the lobby and say, "Shawn, I want you to know that I'm totally on board with the vision, but I'm struggling with your leadership, teaching, communication style, music style, small group structure, etc."

The truth is that all programming needs to be aligned with the vision. If that's true, and someone is complaining about an aspect of the program, they're not fully aligned. For example, the music is aligned with whom we're trying to reach; so if someone is complaining about the music, they're revealing that they're not fully on board with the vision.

We need to call it what it is. They either don't understand how the programming is aligned with the vision, or they're willfully choosing to be misaligned. We need to help bring these people into alignment by clearly communicating how our programming and structure decisions serve our vision.

Let's help people see the forest for the trees. Let's help them to understand that all small parts work to support the whole. You may have to say something like, "You've got to support our strategy, our structure, and our programming in order to fully support the vision, and we need that from you."

STRATEGY 5: BE CAREFUL SELECTING LEADERS.

There's a reason some of your leaders have worked for many companies, but are no longer there. There's a reason they're *former* pastors. There's a reason they taught a large class at their last organization, and they're not doing that now. There's a reason for the discrepancy between their resume and their current status.

So many times, we're impressed by first impressions, and we lay our hands on leaders too quickly. In the apostle Paul's writings to his mentee, Timothy, he tells Timothy to be cautious in selecting new leaders. In my life, I've made bad decisions. Many times, these scenarios played out across a Starbucks table. I said, "Hey, I like you! Why don't you come work for me?" Most of the time, these relationships didn't end well. Many other leaders have told me, "I pulled the trigger too quickly. I let a resume impress me and I got into trouble."

We tend to hire too fast and fire too slowly. Rarely does a leader say, "Wow, I probably let them go too quickly." But countless leaders have said, "I wish I'd have taken care of that a long time ago." Be careful selecting new leaders. Ask questions about your programming, your strategy, your structure, and your values. Get multiple people involved in the interview process—this applies to volunteers and paid staff.

Every leader we select in an organization must be willing and capable to become a torchbearer of the vision. If they can't, or won't do that, it doesn't matter how much capacity they have; they'll be toxic in your culture, in your organization, and with your vision. We have to make sure prospective team members are on board with the vision before we select them.

STRATEGY 6: SAY NO EARLY, AND OFTEN.

Somewhere along the way, we began believing that to be a good Christian you have to say yes to everything and everyone. This is not what Jesus did. How many times did Jesus try to get away from people so that He could focus on why He truly came to earth?

Read Mark 1:35-39. Crowds are lining up to get to Him, to be healed, and to hear Him preach. Instead, Jesus says, "No. We've got to go on to the next town, and preach the gospel there. That is why I came." He knew His purpose.

Leaders need to stretch our "no" muscles! Repeat after me: "No, we're not going to be able to do that." Go ahead—say it out loud! Did you do it? Great. Now, practice that ten or fifteen times a day, and you'll get better at it.

You can always say yes later if needed. It's easier to say no now and yes later than it is to say yes now and no later. It's much more difficult to shut something down on the back end than to say no on the front end. It can be awkward to say no; but if you wait until it's too late, it causes damage. Choose awkwardness over damage. Say no early, and often.

STRATEGY 7: HAVE THE COURAGE TO LET PEOPLE GO.

Not everyone is going to make it all the way with you. Some people are going to leave. You're in good company; this happened to Jesus, too. He sought twelve, and one didn't make it. You're going to invest everything you have into your people. You're going to spend countless hours, days, months—maybe years—on them, and some of them are not going to make it.

Sometimes, leaders think they're "one hire away from growth." Instead, we are often "one fire away from growth." If there's a weak link in the chain—a toxic person, a Debbie Downer, a wet blanket—someone who just doesn't get it, you *have* to deal with it. Patrick Lencioni says that one of the five dysfunctions of a team is inattention to results. John Michael claims that the problem in too many ministries today is, "We have ushers that can't ush and Suzies that can't sing, and we won't tell them."

We owe our team members four things: grace, honesty, proper placement, and prayer. We owe our organizations these things, as well. We are stewards of the organizations and the people in them, so we must ensure we have the right people in the right seats at the right time.

Can I encourage you? I know you've had losses. I know you've had people leave and had their spouse defriend your spouse on Facebook. I know this happens all the time. It's happened to me, too. Some people will come with you, and others will go. Rarely do the ones who start with you finish with you. So what do you need to do? Don't beg everyone to stay. I've never been able to talk someone into staying. Have the courage to let them go. Do your best to leave people better than you found them; and when they leave, focus on the ones still with you. They have stayed! That's a miracle to consider. Despite all our leadership shortcomings, some are still with us! Don't focus on what's been lost. Reassemble the army if necessary, and get to the next level.

STRATEGY 8: LIVE FOR AN AUDIENCE OF ONE.

How are you going to accomplish all seven of these strategies, and ensure your vision doesn't get hijacked? The answer is simple: by living for an audience of One. That's the only way to stand up to the daily pressure.

Live for your Master, who is away but is coming back. When He gets back, He'll want us to give an account of how we've stewarded our visions. If we've been faithful, we'll be blessed for it—we'll hear, "Well done, good and faithful servant." That's why we lead. That's why you do what you do. That's why you can go back into the trenches and be mean about the vision.

chapter 9

ALIGNMENT AS A KEY TO ELEVATION

ZAKIYA LARRY

STARTED OUT IN THE newsroom as a reporter and producer, working for radio and television. I've worked for Public Radio International and National Public Radio, and also have experience in corporate communications and public relations. I've spent 15 years in the communications industry, developing the concepts I'm about to share with you. I have seen these concepts in action, and I believe they can change your life!

Today, I'm an elevation strategist. I help elevate brands, moods, and ideas through strategic public relations, media coaching, and keynote speaking. Business leaders, entrepreneurs, politicians, athletes, and other individuals come to me, and I help to align them for success.

Regardless of your field or your goals, I trust you are looking to expand. You want to expand your territory, your customer base, and your visibility. I've had the great fortune of working in the faith-based arena from a strategic public relations perspective for many years. In that time, I've met many global marquee faith leaders. One thing I hear consistently in the ministry sphere is, "I know what God has called me to do. I know what I have. How do I get more people to interact with what we're doing here in our ministry?"

This question isn't exclusive to ministry; people are also asking it in the marketplace: "We have a great product. We have a great service. How do we get more people to hear about us?" How do you get more people to see and buy in to what you're doing? I'm going to give you three key points that answer that question. My desire is to help you to align yourself with power players in other industries, in order to equip you to elevate your brand, your business, and your ministry for success.

KEY POINT NUMBER 1: ALIGNMENT
Align yourself with your target audience.

If you want to grow your brand beyond its current borders, you need to identify your target audience. You may be thinking, "I know who my customer is—I've done my research." If you're in ministry, you may think, "I know the demographics of my Sunday attendees. We have a grasp on what they like, what they need, and who they are." It's critical to know those you serve.

However, when we're talking about going from where you are to where you want to be, you need to reach additional people—*your new, expanded target audience.* Who are *they*? Before you can reach them through public relations and media, you need to figure out who, and where, they are.

Whom do you want to reach? You are vision-setting and goal-casting for a new audience. Ask yourself these necessary questions:

Where do they live?

How old are they?

What work do they do?

What do they need?

What do they enjoy?

What's important to them?

What attracts them?

What are they already doing?

How do they relax?

What do they do for fun?

Once you've identified who these people are, you can start aligning your business or ministry to them in order to draw them in to what you're doing. How does this process work? Ask yourself, "What are other organizations doing that is successful with this audience?" Are you trying to attract Millennials? What messages are other businesses using to pull them in? Do you want more men in your ministry? Do you see something in another ministry that is really attracting fathers? Take time and invest effort in researching what products, messages, and services are already working with your new audience.

Additionally, take inventory of what's working with those you're already reaching. How might you expand those strategies to influence a greater audience? Is there anything working now that might *not* work with a greater audience? What might you need to change?

It's so important to align yourself with your new audience. This doesn't just encompass your practices—it includes your brand.

Align your brand.

Have you created a solid, memorable brand for yourself? Sometimes, it's easier for leaders to think in terms of vision or mission than it is to think about brand. This is okay. Your mission statement or vision includes who you are, what you do, why you do it, and often, where you'd like to go. This is all the foundation for your brand. If your mission statement doesn't include whom you want to impact, you'll need to figure that out by establishing your brand.

Everyone uses the word "brand"—it's one of the most overused words in public relations. But many people are misdefining the word. When they think "brand," they think of their logo, the marquee outside their building, or their website. By the time you're picking out colors for a logo, the train has already left the building. These things are only the visual expressions of your brand.

Your brand is a promise. Circle that. Highlight it. Remember it. Write it on a sticky note and put it on your computer monitor. In order to be aligned for success—in order to align to your different audiences—you have to make sure your brand is in line. Ask yourself, "What do people experience when they interact with me? What do people get from me, my staff, and my organization? Are they getting that consistently? Are we improving, or becoming less reliable?"

Whatever folks experience the most when they interact with you is your promise—and your brand. Things that are consistent with a brand become embedded in people's minds. Those people automatically associate their expectations of you with your brand. If your brand has something that needs changing, change it! You don't want negative promises embedded in your audience's minds!

This change takes work. I tell my clients all the time: "Before you invite people over for dinner, make sure the kitchen is clean." This same principle applies to greater visibility. So many organizations would love to have more attention. They'd love to be on TV, and featured in newspapers and magazines...but their kitchen isn't clean. Their brand's promise isn't aligned with the image they want to present. If this is you, ask yourself this question: "What small tweaks can I make to improve the purity of my promise?" You may need to improve the way your staff interacts with people, or the way your customers are greeted at the door, or your programs. Your promise is your foundation, so make sure it's aligned with the image you want to project, as well as the audience you want to attract. You want a cohesive, polished brand that elevates your company for greater visibility.

KEY POINT NUMBER 2: POSITIONING

Let's say you've identified a new target audience, and you have a nice synergy going in terms of creating your brand. What do you do next?

Positioning is key for the growth of any organization. Essentially, positioning is creating a formula that shapes how people think and feel about you, your product, or your organization. Positioning establishes people's perception of you. When I work with organizations, I often help establish their new positioning. I worked with a pastor who was known as a great preacher, but he wanted to reach a new audience—a secular audience. His brand communicated that he was in ministry, that he was a skilled and experienced preacher; however, if he wanted to transition to being a national thought leader, he had to align his brand with his new target audience, thereby creating new positioning for himself. It was my job to find a way to position this person in different arenas and with different language, so that people understood there was more to his platform than Sunday mornings.

If you have a goal to move beyond the pulpit, or beyond your current borders, positioning is the way to do it. Identify where you want to go, and create a framework around that. Then, place yourself within that framework.

There are two components to effective positioning: effective language and practical positioning.

First, there's language. You need a clear, strong statement with language that helps people understand the arenas in which you operate. Here's what that might look like: My pastoral client went from "Minister X pastors at Church XYZ" to "Joe Lewis not only pastors at Church XYZ, but also leads lectures, and mentors men, on the following topics."

See what just happened? This is a brand shift with new positioning. We took him beyond the typical purview of what a minister does. Now, his audience thinks, "If I'm interested in Sunday mornings, then he's the guy"; but they *also* think, "I'm interested in being mentored. I'm a man and I have questions, and I just heard this is the go-to guy!"

Sometimes, we think that if we pitch a big tent, we'll cover all that we do. If we say, "We're a full service agency," people will automatically assume that we offer what they're seeking. This isn't true. They won't understand. That language is too ambiguous. Instead of having a broad, inclusive meaning, it has no meaning at all. It's up to you and your team to use precise language that clearly establishes your position. Speak directly to your target audience in a language they'll hear and understand.

Once you've got your language down, you need to practically put yourself in the right places at the right times. You've worked hard to find, and align to, your target audience. Now, position yourself where they are. You may need to put yourself in new places that help you shift your current brand. Don't forget to communicate about these new places so that people know where to find you.

Let's say you're a phenomenal cupcake baker who wants to get into wedding cakes. You need to move your speaking engagements outside of just cupcake festivals. Start pitching yourself at wedding venues and expos. Go where the people are, and let them know that you're ready, willing, and equipped to meet their needs. Don't simply pitch a big tent and tell people you can do any and all baking; instead, position yourself as an expert wedding cake producer.

Here's another example. Let's say you're a successful local singer who's found that you have a gift for songwriting. Continue performing your own material at your established gigs; but in addition, join songwriter's circles. Let people know you're available to lead songwriting workshops. Once you're properly positioned, you can begin to think about letting the whole world know who you are.

KEY POINT NUMBER 3: VISIBILITY

Sometimes, people are most excited about this piece of the puzzle; however, I hope you didn't skip ahead to get here, because you need to take care of alignment and positioning before you can expand your visibility. You must master your message before you can master your media.

It's not enough to want to be seen. It's not enough to draw eyes to your company or ministry. In fact, if you gain visibility without doing the groundwork, it can absolutely derail your goals. The closer you get to the spotlight, the hotter it gets. You need solid alignment and positioning so that, if your message gets muddied, you can come back to center, stand on your firmly established brand and in your firmly established position, and clarify who you are and what you offer.

Visibility can mean multiple things, but it's always about reaching a greater audience. Depending on your industry, this could mean increasing your customer base, reaching more people in your ministry, or increasing your bottom line. To gain visibility, you will need to reach out to media outlets that operate in your geographical region and in your areas of interest.

Take a look around your city and region and determine:

- Are they covering the types of stories I care about?
- Could I be a spokesperson for the issues they cover?
- Do they report on types of stories I am already doing in-house with my ministry or company?
- Do they know about me? Should they?

Look at media outlets that align with what you do and what you have to offer. A wedding planner needs to be featured in bridal magazines, not hunting ones. The hunting guide needs to be featured in hunting magazines, not bridal ones. Choose media outlets that are friendly to what you have to offer. If you're a liberal organization, you don't want to approach a conservative media out-let—unless, of course, you are looking for a debate.

With these thoughts in mind, create a list of media properties: radio, television, newspapers, and mag-azines. Don't forget to strategically approach social media. Choose outlets that align with your goals and vision. Then, use your brand and positioning to clearly and powerfully communicate to these outlets who you are, what you do, and why they should interact with you and your events. You don't just want them to list your events. You want them to attend your events and actively be a part of them.

A public relations professional can help open doors and form connections with the right people. My team and I do this. If you can't afford professional help, you can do this groundwork yourself. It's not easy, but it is effective—in part because, when you connect with these professionals, you get to borrow their credibility.

When you see a Ford commercial on television, you know that Ford paid an actor to climb behind the wheel and look excited. They paid someone to shoot and edit that film, and they paid someone to show it on the air. This is effective advertising, but everyone knows it's advertising—paid for by the product being advertised. However, when you sit down in front of the cameras with a well-liked reporter, there's an element of trust between the audience and the program. That reporter is a professional and has credibility that he or she then lends to you. The audience sees you as a real entity, not just another bit of paid programming.

Even today, when the integrity of some news sources is being questioned, people generally still respect media outlets and know that they're supposed to be objective. Otherwise, news outlets wouldn't have their audiences. If you're being featured by a news outlet that aligns with your brand, you'll reach an audience who finds that outlet credible. This results in a subconscious endorsement that's worth more than money can buy.

Speaking of buying, many organizations focus solely on placing ads, buying banners, and telling people to pick up the newest book. This is marketing. Marketing and public relations run on parallel tracks, but they're different. Marketing is used to sell. Public relations shapes public opinion. There's value in both, and each can drive the other. However, they are still different and, therefore, require different efforts. You want to drive your bottom line (marketing), but you also want to attract people who know, approve of, and trust you—those who will be loyal and join you in efforts to reach your goals. These eager, committed fans may even help you reach that burning passion deep inside that God has given you—that thing you've been built to carry.

In order to reach these people and create this buy-in, you've got to manage the public's understanding of who you are and what you do. As you increase your visibility, the promise of your brand grows stronger, which allows you to create more effective positioning, which results in greater visibility. These keys—alignment (with audience and with brand), positioning, and visibility—all work together in a powerful cycle that increases your success. Studies show that, on average, people need to encounter something seven times before it even registers. This is a marathon, not a sprint.

Word of mouth was the original form of public relations, and it still works today. Following this cyclical formula will shift how people think. Eventually, they'll give you that word of mouth endorsement without you having to push and beg.

So align your company with the brand you want, and align that brand with your new audience. Then, position yourself where and when your target audience will find you. Finally, work on your visibility. Get yourself seen by your target audience in ways that align with who you are and what you have to offer. This will skyrocket your brand to meet, and exceed, your goals.

chapter 10

THE IMPORTANCE OF KEEPING SCORE

DEANDRE SALTER

WHEN WE THINK ABOUT alignment for success, there's one critical factor that ensures any organization is successful. Simply put, it's keeping score. It amazes me how few leaders in business, ministry, and nonprofits keep score. Even fewer keep score consistently, and an even smaller group actually hold themselves accountable for the results.

Here's a critical question I want us to wrestle with in our work: "Am I keeping score in my business/ministry?" Are you consistently measuring your progress, and holding yourself and your team accountable for the results? If not, that's why you're reading this. As a leader, if you don't keep track of things, you'll cost your team a win.

I love all sports, but I'm particularly fond of the NCAA tournament every March. If you're a college basketball fan, you've seen time and time again how coaches' and star players' unaware decisions can cost their team the win. The most famous instance of this may be the Chris Webber timeout in the championship game of Michigan versus North Carolina. It all began when Pat Sullivan, a starter for North Carolina, made the first of two free throws. He gave North Carolina a 73-71 lead. There were only 20 seconds left, and Sullivan, feeling the pressure on the second shot, flubbed it. That handed Michigan a shot to tie the game, or win it. Chris Webber, a team captain for Michigan, grabbed the rebound, raced down the court, ran down the sideline, and frantically looked around for an open teammate. He was surrounded by Tar Heel arms. There were 11 seconds left, and the Wolverines had already used their final timeout. Nevertheless, Webber put his right palm over the top of his left fingers and called a timeout.

Now, the problem was that his team was out of timeouts. This resulted in a technical fine, which gave North Carolina a chance for another free throw. Chris Webber cost his team the game because he was not keeping track of the timeouts his team had left. He's not alone. Many of us, if we're honest, have made similar decisions that have cost our team and our organization wins, simply because we weren't situationally aware. We weren't measuring for results. Because we weren't keeping score, our team suffered.

Today, we want to make a shift in this kind of behavior. If you're a leader, I know you're reading this because your passion and your call is strong. We don't want to lose out on our big visions because of technical fines. Jesus speaks to this topic in Luke 14:28-30:

Suppose one of you wants to build a tower. Won't you first sit down and estimate the cost to see if you have enough money to complete it? For if you lay the foundation and are not able to finish it, everyone who sees it will ridicule you, saying, "Who's this person who began to build and wasn't able to finish?"

I love this passage, because the revelations are manifold. First, we see there's a cost associated with being great at what we do. In the context of Luke 14, we find that Jesus wants the large crowds following Him to understand that there is a difference between a follower and a disciple. Followers don't pay a price, but disciples do. Why? Because disciples are leaders. Second, Jesus shares that disciple leaders are situationally aware. They actually keep score. They sit down and estimate the cost of building a tower beforehand, to make sure there's enough money to finish the project. This is where I'd like us to take a deeper look. This is a massive verse, with so much practical application for all leaders.

Let's get to the bottom line. Jesus is concluding that one should not do anything without measuring. Simply put, why should I do anything without keeping score? In fact, Jesus says that these people should manage their tower building in such a way that there's actually money left over in their budget. At an organizational level, that sounds like profit. At a personal level, that sounds like savings.

Jesus says we have to measure things that are important. We have to measure things if we want to achieve vision. He wants His followers to measure the cost of being a disciple, not to scare them away, but to make sure they understand what it will take to be successful at discipleship. Likewise, I'm urging leaders today to make sure you align your organizations for success by challenging yourself, and your team, to measure results—to keep score. That's actually one of the costs of leadership.

Many leaders operate without quantifiable goals and objectives. When this is the case, they're literally operating in the dark. Keeping score accomplishes four things: it increases our commitment, it increases accountability, it increases our motivation and drive, and it increases the level of our teamwork. Allow me to share a few thoughts concerning each of these accomplishments.

KEEPING SCORE INCREASES COMMITMENT.

Keeping score forces leaders to commit to making hard, necessary decisions. Honestly, I believe many leaders don't keep score because they're uncomfortable with holding people's feet to the proverbial fire for results. I'm a fan of a particular football team. I'm not going to mention any names, but I've been a fan of this team since I was a little boy. My whole life, our team has won championships, but we've also been mediocre and missed the playoffs quite a bit. Here's the key difference between the times my team was winning and when it was mediocre:

When we were winning championships, we had coaches committed to keeping score of every team member—every player, every coach. When we were losing, we hired coaches that didn't drive commitment. In fact, they knew the numbers. They had a scorecard; but they didn't have the guts to make hard decisions that would bolster commitment. Under these coaches, if a player underperformed, no one tracked how many hours they spent watching film; no one held them accountable to how many extra practices they did. These coaches weren't tracking players. The players seemed to never pay a price for questionable off-the-field behaviors. There were games like this when I'd scream at the television.

Team building doesn't have to make concession to team complacency. Ministry leaders: I know you have a heart for ministry and people. I understand that you feel like you shouldn't always manage the church like the world manages; and to some extent that may be true. But there are certain universal management principles at play. In other words, the idea that we must monitor performance and hold people accountable at every level is quite universal. It's what Jesus was getting at in Luke 14. Having a scorecard allows us to make decisions based upon the facts, not just the heart.

I'm not suggesting that there's no role for heart, but I am suggesting that there's no place for heart without facts. You've got to keep score of your staff. If you've coached them, and they're still not responding, you have to do the hard thing and move in another direction—not simply move the problem to another department or ministry. This is all so that you can get back to what Jesus was speaking about, which is finishing the tower.

Keeping score increases commitment because it allows us to change for the better. Numbers don't lie. Jesus used the phrase, "You must sit down," implying "do your homework before building a tower." Once you do the cost-benefit analysis and really let the numbers speak truth, you'll be able to make better strategic decisions. The confidence level of an organization increases when everyone understands the numbers. People often misrepresent the truth, but numbers never do.

There's a higher level of commitment and buy-in when we show evidence for our decisions. If we're to align our organizations for success, we must lead by evidence and not lead by antidote. If you're going to make decisions, make sure the numbers support those decisions. Jesus says, "Sit down. Write it out. Believe the numbers." Many more people would be committed to getting better at what they do if they really understood their bottom line. As a leader, that's what you're charged with doing: helping your team understand the value of keeping score.

KEEPING SCORE INCREASES ACCOUNTABILITY.

Keeping score also allows leaders to make their teams accountable for whether their hard work is profitable. An expensive habit is one in which you're losing money and ground consistently. While this may be okay for recreational matters, it's not what God has called us to as leaders. We ought to hear Jesus' words in Luke 14 and avoid making our enterprises merely expensive habits.

Profitability may be the primary measure of effectiveness. It's the only thing that allows us to continue doing what we do. If you're a pastor, and there's nothing left for the future vision God has given you, your doors might not be open next Sunday. If you own a business today and you're not managing to profit, your shop might not be open next week.

When we look at Paul's teaching on church leadership in 1 Timothy 3, we see that he says leaders in the church ought to be good managers, both at home and in the church. In fact, Paul argues that, if one can't manage well at home, that person will also have trouble managing at church. The word for "manage" here implies more than simply being a good leader; it actually implies one who is adept at administration.

Administration includes stewardship of your family's finances (and, likewise, the church's finances). Our society's consumerism is at an all-time high. In fact, the most recent statistics show that the average American has less than $2,000 in their bank account. That same average American has over $16,000 in credit card debt. I fear that many churches and businesses are managing their financial affairs just like the average American: accumulating debt and maintaining very little savings or profit for future vision. This can only happen when no one is keeping score and holding the entire group accountable for profitable results.

Keeping score also helps us identify potential abuse of expenses. It helps us figure out ways to make people accountable, because some of our employees manage their corporate expenses like their personal expenses—with little regard for the bottom line. There must be procedures in place to ensure that the organization's money is used in a way that moves the vision forward. Expense abuse is usually not intentional, but if no one's watching the corporate coffers, the team could be staying at the Four Seasons when, actually, they should be staying at the Four Points Motel.

KEEPING SCORE INCREASES MOTIVATION AND DRIVE.

As I mentioned earlier, I'm a big sports fan. Here's the one thing all sports have in common: they keep score. Why? Because they're motivated to win. If there's no scorecard, there's no winner or loser; and if there's no winner or loser, there's no motivation to try harder. People love being a part of a winning story.

If you have a vision God has called you to, and you want to achieve it, you need to have a scorecard and share the results with your team. You want to lead your team to win. You want to win souls. You want to win customers. You want to win contracts or grants. But organizations that don't keep score are usually underperforming. Everyone gets motivated when they have a chance to win. It's your job as the leader to make sure that your team understands what's at stake.

Keeping score isn't threatening. It simply allows everyone to see what needs to be done to win the game. It's motivating to know that, "If we do X, then Y will happen. We only need one more point this quarter to win!" This knowledge motivates teams to exceed our past performances and to reach for broader goals. It lets us set measurable benchmarks and look at our historical performance to see how we compete against ourselves. Nobody's going to take your business seriously if you're not keeping score. Likewise, no one is going to take a leader seriously if they're not situationally aware of pitfalls.

KEEPING SCORE INCREASES TEAMWORK.

The last thing I want to tell you about keeping score is that it increases teamwork. Knowing and managing for the score empowers a team to work well together. It allows your team to form creative solutions that drive specific action plans. It allows us to lead our team members to outcomes and results from the ideas and projects that we put forward. This ends up pushing our whole team forward with a performance-driven culture. People are likely to work hard when they understand clearly how their work matters. This is why keeping score increases teamwork—it allows us to recognize, with appreciation, our best employees, volunteers, and donors.

When you have numbers, you can identify those who really make the organization prosper. It's a good idea to never take these people for granted. Find a way to offer them some sort of recognition or reward—maybe a vacation, a dinner, or a day off when they reach a specific goal. This makes everyone feel like they're part of the win. That's why, in professional sports, every member gets a championship ring. Each of them had a part to play, and made a contribution. They are recognized and celebrated for what they've contributed.

Now, I didn't discuss specific scorekeeping procedures. There are probably many different types of leaders reading this right now, all of whom may need something a bit unique. Rather than get into specifics, I'd like to share with you a few tips on how you can keep score, and the most important thing that every leader should track.

Don't track everything. Not only is it tedious, but it can be ineffective and distract you from your larger mission. When Jesus says, "Do an estimate," He's clearly speaking to measurements, materials and costs. Does one need to measure the number of leaves on the ground to come up with an estimate for building a tower? No. That level of detail is interesting, but it's just not important. Let's not fall into the booby-trap of measuring things for measurement's sake. Here's a simple rule of thumb: If you cannot make a strategic shift based upon the information you're tracking, it's not important. Just let it go. I know you want to know how many people in blue shirts walked through your doors at 10:00 a.m., but what will you do with that information? If nothing, let it go.

At one point, as a pastor, I had my team measure average baptisms per Sunday for almost a year, until it dawned on me that we only have baptism once a month. In other words, the average baptism for three to four Sundays is zero. There was nothing we could change on a week-to-week basis. Ultimately, I changed the measurement to a monthly one so I could actually develop actionable items instead of trying to track it weekly, which was a waste of time.

We need to start by tracking what Jesus says everyone should track: profit. Profitability drives us, and provides a future of financing for our vision. Here's a simple technique to develop your own profit scorecard: it's called the "5 Whys" technique. It was developed by Toyota to improve their manufacturing process, so that they could become more competitive in the global automotive marketplace. I use this principle for developing my own scorecards for the various teams and organizations I lead.

The "5 Whys" technique starts with the measurement. We develop answers, and then we ask five levels of why. For example, if your measurement is, "Are we printable this month?" the answer may be yes or no. The second level includes deeper questions, such as, "Why are we or aren't we profitable?" The answer to this question could possibly identify an expense or income issue; or perhaps the organization has both. Either way, you now have a new score to keep track of (tracking income and expenses on a month-to-month basis, for instance). The third level of "Why" could include a question such as, "Why do we have an income or an expense issue?" The answer could be that a certain expense item is too high. Whatever the issue is, asking why at a third level creates a brand new metric (perhaps looking at the numbers of new customers and new guests, in this case).

Of course, I could go on through levels four and five, but you get the picture. Rather than simply tracking what everyone else is tracking, I'm encouraging you to track the scores that matter to your particular business or ministry. Start getting unstuck today. Only by keeping a scorecard can you empower your organization, get aligned for success, fix what's broken, and get back on track.

I want to close with four empowering questions for you to consider. The first question is, "What do you keep score on; what's important to your organization's success?" The second is, "Are you the only person in your organization keeping score, or do you challenge others to keep score?" Third, "Who are other leaders in your organization who should be keeping their own scores, and how are you coaching them to do so?" Last, "Have you and your team discussed the key metrics that are critical to achieving your success?"

In Luke 14, Jesus continues. He says, "For if you lay the foundation and are not able to finish it, everyone who sees it will ridicule you, saying, 'This person began to build and wasn't able to finish.'"

My point is that simple. We represent the King of kings, and He wants us to finish the work we've started. He wants us to achieve the vision He's given each of us. He wants us to lead our people to that place. He doesn't want us to be ridiculed because we didn't sit down and estimate the cost. Jesus wants us to plan, measure, and track performance so that we finish—as disciples, as church leaders, and as business leaders. If we follow His advice, I believe our organizations will soar to higher heights.

So I encourage you today: know the score. Win the game. Begin to answer those empowering questions; develop your leaders; develop your team; figure out for your own organization, beyond profit, the five levels you need to track. If you do those things, you'll do exactly what Jesus says—you'll finish well.

chapter 11

REALIGNING YOUR PERSPECTIVE

MARTIJN VAN TILBORGH

LIGNING YOURSELF FOR SUCCESS begins with aligning your perspective. You must align what you see, from where you are, with what God sees from where He is. As mere humans, we have a limited perspective. Your perspective determines whether or not you're going to shrink your leadership capacity or expand it.

When you align your perspective with God's, you'll expand your leadership capacity immensely. I want to give you some tools that will help you do just that. Let's start by looking at Isaiah 30:23:

He will also send you rain for the seed you sow in the ground, and the food that comes from the land will be rich and plentiful.

God will give the rain for your seed. What an interesting Scripture! Isaiah mentions two specific things here: rain and seed—both of which are necessary for harvest. The seed represents the Word of God. God's Word is powerful. It can change things. The Word of God is truth; the Word of God is revelation. However, in order for the Word to bear fruit and not remain dormant, we need the rain.

It doesn't matter whether you're a business leader or a ministry leader—it's all part of God's kingdom. You're a leader, and God has declared a specific word over your life. He has a design that will bring you to a place where you can fulfill your purpose. But in order for that specific word to start bearing fruit and producing a harvest, one thing has to happen: rain. That's what this verse from Isaiah says. God will give you the rain that your seed needs so it can produce abundance. Simply having a word over your life doesn't mean anything. A seed can lie dormant for a long time; but as God releases the rain, a harvest comes.

So the question is, "How do we get rain?" Scripture tells us, "Then He will give rain." When I see the word "then" in Scripture, I ask, "When?" We need to go back in Scripture and see what God means when He says, "Then."

In previous verses, Isaiah explains what triggers, what unleashes, what releases the rain. Look at verse 22:

Then you will desecrate your idols overlaid with silver and your images covered with gold; you will throw them away like a menstrual cloth and say to them, "Away with you!"

Isaiah is talking about the images we create and elevate as idols. This relates to our perspective. Our perspective determines what images we create. Our limited viewpoint can lead us to create images that are foreign to the image of God—images not in line with His perspective. Isaiah says we've got to cast these images out, to say to them, "Be gone!" *Then* God will release the rain to our seed. If we want to see the fulfillment of prophecy—if we want to see the Word of God over our lives—we need to deal with the false images we've created.

Think about the story of Exodus: Moses leads his people out of Egypt. They get to Mount Horeb, and God appears before His people—and His people are terrified. God descends onto the mountain with an earthquake and thunder and lightning, and the Israelites freak out. "Moses! We can't listen to this guy! If we listen to Him, we will surely die!" They couldn't handle the manifestation of God in their lives.

In that moment, the people decided to transfer the leadership responsibility to Moses. "Moses, why don't you go up the mountain and listen to God? Why don't you take the risk? And then you come back down, and we'll do whatever it is He told you to do." They created an intermediary who would speak to God on their behalf. They removed themselves from all risk: the thunder, the shaking, and the darkness. They no longer had to deal with all of that, because they transferred the responsibility from themselves to Moses. They no longer needed to modify their own perspective.

But there was a problem. They had decided they weren't going to listen to God; they were going to listen to Moses. But Moses was missing. He was gone for forty days. So they went to Aaron and said, "We need something to give expression to a genuine experience we had as we came out of Egypt." There's the deception. Out of a genuine encounter with God, they created a golden calf. From their limited perspective, they tried to express something they didn't understand and created an idol.

They had been slaves in Egypt and, by supernatural intervention, had gotten out of Egypt. That deliverance was real. It was authentic. God had truly delivered them. But then, they came to a place where they had to give expression to their faith, and they couldn't because they did not maintain the genuine relationship with God. Instead, they said, "We want something like other people have: something tangible." Hence, the golden calf.

Isn't this interesting? The molded image is the result of a genuine experience with God. We see, then, that it's possible to have a true encounter with God, yet misrepresent Him in our actions. The Israelites weren't saying, "Here's a golden calf that has nothing to do with Yahweh." No, they molded an image and *called it Yahweh*. As a kid, I always thought these Israelites deviated from their belief and started worshipping another God; but it wasn't that simple. They claimed that their molded image had delivered them out of Egypt. They'd had a real experience, with the real God, but they misrepresented Him.

We leaders today have also created images that misrepresent God. God wants us to deal with these so that He can expand our leadership capacity. As Isaiah says, when we remove these images, rain will be released so that we can bear fruit from the seed, the word that God has planted in our spirits.

Isaiah 43:18-19 tells us more about having a Godly perspective:

"Remember ye not the former things, neither consider the things of old. Behold, I will do a new thing; now it shall spring forth; shall ye not know it? I will even make a way in the wilderness, and rivers in the desert." (KJV)

God is about to do a new thing, but there's a prerequisite. We can't experience a new thing of God unless one thing happens. God said, "Do not remember the former things or the old things." The "former things," the "old things," are the way we've always done things, the way we've always seen things. Looking back at these keeps us from experiencing the new thing God has for us. Our old perspective shrinks our leadership capacity. It keeps us from truly leading people to a place of freedom—a place where they can fulfil their God-given purpose.

People have argued with me about the "new thing" part of this Scripture, saying, "There is nothing new under the sun." Of course this is true. There is nothing new under the sun, because God knows the end before the beginning. He created us before we were born. We have a purpose that He's already declared over our lives. All of that is true about God's perspective. But we don't know any of this unless God reveals it to us. So, for us, it is very much *a new thing*. If we are going to expand our leadership capacity, we must receive revelation from God—revelation that expands our perspective.

People have said to me, "You're an innovator, so that's why you're able to think that way." I tell them that we are *all* innovators by divine design. Each of us is unique. There is only one you. There are unique attributes to your call, to your purpose, that are unique to you. If you're truly walking in your purpose, you will give birth to something completely unique. That makes you an innovator!

Now, when you interrupt the status quo, you will rock the boat. It doesn't matter if you're dealing with the status quo in church, in business, or elsewhere—if you're trying to move the world, as people know it, forward, you have to start doing things differently. Innovation always happens on the edge of chaos; that's how you know you're truly being innovative. The fact that there's chaos simply means that no one has gone there before.

So, if we're part of the status quo, and God wants to do something new in our lives, this creates a conflict. God's innovation conflicts with what's already established. But this chaos serves a purpose: it stretches us so we can come into new possibilities. And we're going to need these possibilities if we're going to expand our leadership capacity. We can't get the new perspective we need if we don't go through this chaos.

Exodus 6:3 shows us that perspective has everything to do with information, with revelation:

I appeared to Abraham, to Isaac and to Jacob as God Almighty, but by my name the Lord I did not make myself fully known to them.

Think about this for a moment. These three men played crucial roles in history, and God revealed Himself to each of them. However, by their limited perspective, they understood Him as God Almighty. They did *not* understand Him as Lord. Even though God *is* Lord, that information was not part of their perspective.

It's possible to know God in one way, but not another. So when God reveals Himself in a way that's outside our paradigm—when He gives us new information and a new perspective, it rocks the boat. It expands us. We see more of Him, and therefore, we can be better leaders.

Let's look at a practical example. We've all heard teachings on finances. What Scripture is most quoted in these sermons? Malachi 3:10-11:

Bring ye all the tithes into the storehouse, that there may be meat in mine house, and prove me now herewith, saith the Lord of hosts, if I will not open you the windows of heaven, and pour you out a blessing, that there shall not be room enough to receive it. And I will rebuke the devourer for your sakes, and he shall not destroy the fruits of your ground; neither shall your vine cast her fruit before the time in the field, saith the Lord of hosts (KJV).

Someone becomes a believer, and they hear this message: "Hey, guess what? You're a believer now, so what do you do? Tithe! Why? Because if you don't tithe, the devourer will come, and the windows of heaven will be closed."

I'm not trying to take anything away from that Scripture. It's God's Word. However, maybe our perspective could change regarding these verses. Maybe, through revelation, we could get a higher understanding.

Maybe God shows you another verse, and you think, "Hey, unless the seed falls into the ground and dies, it will not bear fruit," and God starts to reveal to you that, yes, you can continue to tithe out of fear of the devourer; or you could give because you want the seed to die. You're not even thinking about what will happen after you give; you're simply giving because you want to. Suddenly, when it comes to tithing, you have a higher understanding.

But later, perhaps God takes you to a whole new level of understanding. You stopped focusing on the windows, because you wanted the seed to die; but now, God brings your eyes back to the windows and shows you that *you* are that window to the world around you! *You are the window of heaven.* So your perspective shifted from tithing because you're supposed to, to tithing so the seed would die, to tithing as a way of letting heaven's blessings pour out on others. Your perspective has expanded far beyond where you started, and this revelation from God brings tremendous freedom, immense possibilities, and many potential testimonies!

One day, I was walking through the mall, and I saw a dishwasher in an appliance store. I knew someone who needed one, and God said, "I want you to buy it for that person." I became that window of heaven through which blessings poured. Revelation is information that isn't previously known to you. It's not that something suddenly *becomes* true. God's intent with the verses in Malachi hasn't changed. The information was always true, always there; it just wasn't known to me until God revealed it.

Revelation always brings two things: responsibility and change. When God reveals something to you, you are accountable to that new information. What are you going to do with what God has just shown you? If God says, "I want you to be a window of heaven," and if you have a higher understanding of finances, you are accountable to that new knowledge. You must make decisions from your new perspective.

Revelation always causes change. Revelation expands your world. You can see more than you could previously. A leader with an expanded vision must change his or her leadership pattern. Change isn't easy, but it's necessary. If you want to be a game changer, you need to embrace change.

Elisha was a game changer. If we look at his story, we can extract four things that he did that allowed him to be such a leader. Elisha was following Elijah; but one day, Elijah gave Elisha some new information: I'm going to Bethel. You can stay here.

Elijah received this new information and immediately became accountable to it. He knew it was going to bring big change. Here's how he handled this revelation:

Elisha acknowledged the change. He didn't stick his head in the sand and hope the issue would go away.

Elisha embraced the change. He said, "I'm going with you!"

Elisha began to anticipate change. Elijah didn't just go to Bethel. He then went to Jericho and then crossed the Jordan and then went to heaven. That's a lot of changes!

Elisha experienced loss, and put the past behind him.

We would do well to follow this example. When revelation comes, we shouldn't live in denial. We should embrace the change because it came from God. God doesn't just bring one change; He continues to grow us as we allow Him to. We do well to anticipate the changes that will continue to come.

We *must* be willing to experience loss. Remember what God said in Isaiah 43? "Behold, I am doing a new thing. Forget the former things of old. Move on." You're going to lose some images that you molded as a result of your limited perspective. Sometimes, these were big investments. The golden calf certainly was: the people gave up their gold to create that image. We too have invested in images we thought represented God. We must be willing to lose these things and put them behind us. When we do, we become game changers, just like Elisha.

I want to look at one more biblical account. John 5 talks about the pool of Bethesda:

Now there is in Jerusalem by the Sheep Gate a pool, which is called in Hebrew, Bethesda, having five porches. In these lay a great multitude of sick people, blind, lame, paralyzed, waiting for the moving of the water. (NKJV)

A great multitude of people—sick, blind, lame, and paralyzed—waited for the moving of the water. From time to time, an angel would come down and stir the waters, and whoever got there first after the stirring would be healed. This pool is the church. People with limited perspective—lame, blind, deaf—are waiting around for someone to stir the pool so that they can be healed.

One man had been waiting at the pool of Bethesda for 38 years. From his perspective, the only way to get healed was to get into that pool, and he had to wait for someone to carry him in because he couldn't get there without help. This was truth as he understood it, even though Jesus was standing beside him trying to expand his perspective.

The body of Christ is full of lame, blind, paralyzed people waiting around because of their limited perspective of the truth. They have tunnel vision, but God wants to expand their vision. Miracles happened at the pool of Bethesda, but there is a lot more to how God operates than that paradigm. Still, we as a church are lying around the pool waiting, because we don't know there is a larger truth.

John 9 tells us about a different pool—the pool of Siloam—where Jesus healed a man who'd been blind from birth. Isn't that true of all of us—aren't we all born blind? But God wants to give us sight, to give us revelation. He wants to give us new, enlarged perspectives, so we can see and lead. The story of Siloam is one about receiving sight. If we're all lying around the pool of Bethesda, we are looking at the wrong pool! We need to go from the pool of Bethesda to the pool of Siloam, so that we can see. Because when we see, we lead. When we see, we align ourselves with God and His perspective, and we become greater leaders.

chapter 12

JESUS' NEW ALIGNMENT

MATTHEW HESTER

A LIGNMENT BRINGS SUCCESS. Alignment brings benefits into our lives. If we look at the Scriptures, we see profound alignment in the life of Jesus. If it was necessary for Him, we're probably not going to be spared the need for it, either.

The word "aligned" means to arrange in a straight line, to adjust according to that line, and to adjust according to a pattern, or standard. There are tremendous examples of this within the kingdom of God. A prophetic decree of alignment preceded the birth of Jesus. It persisted during His life and continues today, more than two thousand years after His ascension. The life of Jesus constitutes the greatest shift in human history, because His life introduced a fresh alignment concerning the character and nature of the Heavenly Father.

Jesus and His life were marked by a season of tremendous shifts for humanity. In order for these shifts to occur, proper alignment had to be experienced, implemented, and carried out. I want to look at some of the prophetic decrees that came forth many years before Jesus actually came into His earthly ministry. Isaiah wrote:

A voice cries: "In the wilderness prepare the way for the Lord; make straight in the desert a highway for our God." (40:3, ESV)

We could paraphrase this to, "Bring alignment in the desert; make a highway for our God." Isaiah prophetically saw that, before Jesus came, there would be a straight path. There would be a realignment; things would not be the same as they had been before.

Malachi echoes this same idea:

"Behold, I will send my messenger, and he shall prepare the way before me: and the Lord, whom ye seek, shall suddenly come to his temple." (3:1, KJV)

John the Baptist would prepare the way, and then Jesus would come. God is speaking about adjustment here. Things that were misaligned had to be brought into order. Isaiah foresaw this, and then Malachi prophesied the same thing. John the Baptist himself said: "I am the voice of one crying in the wilderness, 'Make straight the way of the Lord', as the prophet Isaiah said" (John 1:23, ESV). The Old Testament prophets knew, as well as John, that Jesus' life on earth was going to bring radical alignment. Once His order was established and His pattern recognized, the world would never be the same.

What path or highway was being made straight for the Lord? To answer this question, we need to ask another: up to this point in history, with what paradigm was the world familiar? Their paradigm had been a system of temple sacrifices and religious observations, with the Pharisees at the helm. The priesthood of that day had lost their true authority.

Then, along comes John the Baptist. Notice that he doesn't cry out, "Jesus is coming to revive the temple system, the sacrifices, and to purify the priesthood." No. He says, "The kingdom of God is at hand." We talk about "radical messages" today, but imagine how radical John the Baptist's message was! No one had been talking of a king and a kingdom in such a way, and here he is claiming that the kingdom is near!

This straight path, this alignment, was threefold in its purpose. First, it dealt with the present reality of the kingdom. The kingdom of God has been a present reality since the days of Jesus, so it has been a present reality for two thousand years. And while it is present, it is still yet to come, because we don't yet see it fully manifested. Second, John's message revealed God as a good Father. Jesus further demonstrated this with His earthly ministry. Up to this point, humankind hadn't looked at God in such a way. They had feared Him.

They'd felt estranged from Him because of the old covenant and the law. Thirdly, this new alignment made possible the finished work of the cross. Everything before the cross made the cross possible—made the perfect redemption achieved there possible.

It's worth noting that, even though John the Baptist was a harbinger for the kingdom of God and the arrival of the Messiah, and even though he cried out for people to get aligned in preparation for these events, he still struggled with personal alignment. John personally witnessed the Holy Spirit descending onto Jesus like a dove. He personally heard God say, "This is my beloved Son in whom I am well pleased."

If I'd been him, at that point, I might have said, "We're closing up shop. My students are becoming your students. My disciples are becoming your disciples, because You are the Messiah!" But that isn't what happened. John continued his own school of discipleship. Shortly before his death, he had doubts about whether Jesus was the promised One. He sent his followers to ask Jesus, "Are you really the one?" Even being John the Baptist, he still had to work on his personal alignment. It's good for us to note this. Even if we carry a message or anointing, we still need to prioritize our spiritual alignment at all times.

Please let me encourage you. When you seek alignment in your organization, business, ministry, or family, don't simply set a standard and ask everyone else to follow it. Sincerely seek alignment for yourself. Yes, God wants you to use your anointing to pour out and bless others, but God also wants you to apply it to your own situation when needed.

So Jesus answered John's men, and then spoke to the crowds about John:

"What did you go out into the wilderness to see? A reed shaken by the wind? What then did you go out to see? A man dressed in soft clothing? Behold, those who are dressed in splendid clothing and live in luxury are in kings› courts. What then did you go out to see? A prophet? Yes, I tell you, and more than a prophet. This is he of whom it is written,

"'Behold, I send my messenger before your face, who will prepare your way before you.'

"'I tell you, among those born of women none is greater than John. Yet the one who is least in the kingdom of God is greater than he." (Luke 7:24-28, ESV)

Talk about a radical shift in perspective! This is a brand new pattern, a new paradigm! With this declaration, Jesus zeroes in on the new alignment He has come to implement, to execute, to release into the world. "We can all agree that John the Baptist is great; but he's of the previous order."

Jesus said, "He's much more than a prophet." I'm reading into what He's saying here, but I think He meant, "The prophets of old looked ahead to me. They looked into the day of the Messiah. They wished they could be here; but John the Baptist is different from them. They saw from afar; he held Me in his hands. He has prepared the way. He brought the baptism of a new order to be released." Jesus made it clear that John the Baptist was *great*, but then He said, "With this new alignment, you can be least and be much greater than John the Baptist." Isn't that something? That's an amazing thing to ponder.

You see, when the disciples of John came to discover who Jesus was, they didn't receive a theological dissertation. I love that. Often, we get sucked into discussions and we try to appeal to people's reason through debate. But Jesus says, "Just tell them what you see." What had John's disciples seen? Tangible evidence of the kingdom of God: diseases healed, plagues cast out, evil spirits driven away. The blind saw. The lame walked. The deaf heard. The dead rose. The poor heard the good news preached to them. Jesus was telling them, "You want to bring him evidence? Tell him that you saw the kingdom of God in action." I imagine that John the Baptist was relieved to receive that report.

With this great shift, these people became exposed to a new idea. The kingdom of God wasn't so much about a king and his subjects as it was about a loving Father and His family. Is God king? Yes, He is; but He's also a good Father. And we know that this is His heart, because this is the relationship He demonstrated to us through the life of Jesus. Jesus didn't come to earth as a slave to the universe; He said, "I'm a Son, a faithful Son; and He's a good father. If you've seen Me, you've seen the Father."

No matter what you've been taught, God is not a belligerent God. He's a good God and a faithful Father. He's looking for kids through whom He can release His blessing and favor and expand His influence. Yes, Jesus is King, but we are not subjects whom He rules. We are a family, and we co-rule with Him. This new, radical alignment, which was reintroduced to humanity with Jesus, was the revelation of the true nature of the kingdom of God. Let's look at three different components to the kingdom of God. Each of these components is a fruit of alignment.

COMPONENT #1: IDENTITY

Identity is born in a place of proper alignment. Once John the Baptist began to preach about kingdom alignment, it was only a matter of time before identity began to be revealed. Jesus was present in the multitude who heard John preach. He desired to be baptized, and it was in this place that the identity of Jesus was released for all the world to witness. Let's look at Matthew 3:13-17:

Then Jesus came from Galilee to the Jordan to John, to be baptized by him. John would have prevented him, saying, "I need to be baptized by you, and do you come to me?" But Jesus answered him, "Let it be so now, for thus it is fitting for us to fulfill all righteousness." Then he consented. And when Jesus was baptized, immediately he went up from the water, and behold, the heavens were opened to him, and he saw the Spirit of God descending like a dove and coming to rest on him; and behold, a voice from heaven said, "This is my beloved Son, with whom I am well pleased." (ESV)

Whom did Jesus find out that He was? He found out that He was beloved and that He was a Son. His identity is no different than yours. You are beloved. You don't have to do anything to earn that. When God declared that Jesus was beloved, Jesus hadn't done anything yet. His ministry hadn't begun, so he hadn't cast out devils or healed the sick. Yet God said, "This is my beloved son." You are also God's beloved son, His beloved daughter. This identity can't be taken from you. God has given it to you. All you have to do is receive it.

COMPONENT #2: RESULTS

When you know who you are, results will follow. First, God secured Jesus' identity with His pronouncement at Jesus' baptism; then, Jesus proved His identity in the wilderness.

The devil didn't drive Jesus into the wilderness; the Spirit did. The Spirit of God drove Jesus into the wilderness to be tested and tempted by the adversary, and each temptation had to do with Jesus' identity: "Are

You who Your Father says You are?" "Do You have what Your Father says You have?" "Can You do what Your Father says You can do?"

Jesus passed the identity test at His baptism; then, He was released into the wilderness to prove the results. Alignment doesn't simply tell you who you are; it also equips you for what you're supposed to do next. Jesus received His identity in an atmosphere of kingdom alignment. He then understood His ministry, and the results would follow once that identity was sure.

Shortly after Jesus' baptism, He travelled to Nazareth. On the Sabbath, He went to the synagogue and read aloud from the scroll of Isaiah:

"The Spirit of the Lord is upon me, because he has anointed me to proclaim good news to the poor. He has sent me to proclaim liberty to the captives and recovering of sight to the blind, to set at liberty those who are oppressed, to proclaim the year of the Lord's favour." (Luke 4:18-19, ESV)

Jesus knew who He was, and He knew what He was supposed to do. He closed the book, handed it off, and said to everyone in the synagogue, "Today this Scripture has been fulfilled in your hearing" (v. 21). He had no doubts about His purpose.

Are you confused about yours? Do you wonder what you're anointed and equipped to do? Alignment answers these questions. If we're off-track, or if our vision is blurry, it's hard to know what we're empowered to do. However, if we understand our identity and embrace the results, we reach our legacy.

COMPONENT #3: LEGACY

Let's be honest: we all want to believe that what we do, what we establish, what we build, and what we carry will be passed on to a generation beyond ourselves. That's Kingdom 101. God is okay with you building something that you enjoy—something that brings you honor; but what we build should outlast us. That's the pattern of the kingdom. It's the pattern Jesus demonstrated for us. It's proper alignment.

This type of alignment serves as a setup for generational blessing and effectiveness. Because Jesus was properly aligned with the standard of the kingdom, it was possible for Him to bring an impartation to His disciples that didn't have to be repaired or adjusted. The previous system—the temple sacrifice system—had proven its flaws many times in the past. Jesus came to establish a new standard.

How many times have we seen powerful ministers or ministries doing great things, and something happens with the leader? Something puts a strain on the ministry, and someone else takes over, only to realize, "There's been so much wrong going on!" It's not always that something was evil—sometimes, there are simply things out of alignment. Maybe an organization's financial structure wasn't aligned. The new leader will then say, "We've got to adjust this if we're going to be successful." This discovery happens all the time in ministries.

This didn't happen in the life of Jesus, because He was perfectly aligned from day one. He knew, "This is my assignment. I embrace it. I know who I am (the identity component), I know what I'm capable of (the results component), and I will leave no stone unturned (the legacy component)."

Let's take a look at the Scripture we call the great commission:

And Jesus came and said to them, "All authority in heaven and on earth has been given to me. Go therefore and make disciples of all nations, baptizing them in the name of the Father and of the Son and of the Holy Spirit, teaching them to observe all that I have commanded you. And behold, I am with you always, to the end of the age." (Matthew 28:18-20, ESV)

All authority has been given to Him. What does "all" mean? "All" means *all. Everything.* If Jesus has all the authority, what's left over? Nothing. So the devil doesn't have any authority. That's not even a question. All authority is given to the Lord; then, He delegates that authority to us. He says, "Go therefore." In the "go," there's an impartation. In the "go," He's transferring that authority to us, His family, and saying, "Continue in the work."

In John 14:12-14, Jesus says this:

*"Truly, truly, I say to you, whoever believes in me
will also do the works that I do; and greater works
than these will he do, because I am going to the
Father. Whatever you ask in my name, this I will do,
that the Father may be glorified in the Son. If you
ask anything in my name, I will do it." (ESV).*

Right there, Jesus says, "When proper alignment
is in place; when you have the kingdom perspective;
when you understand who you are, you won't just do
what I've done..." Sometimes, I joke about this. Most of
us would be content to simply do what Jesus did. But
Jesus said, "This promise goes beyond that. You will
not just do what I've done; you will do greater things!"
Alignment begins to reproduce itself in such a way that
the results become even greater than those of the one
who initially brought this alignment back to earth.

So, as members of the family of God, we have an
amazing responsibility and privilege: to walk in the
fullness of the ministry of Christ. This fullness can
only be found and realized when we properly align
ourselves with the standard of the kingdom. There is
nothing that you can encounter, there is nothing that
you can face, that God has not already equipped and
empowered you to do; but you have to focus on proper alignment.

The things that are out of order in your life: submit
them to the Lord. Go before Him with a heart of repen-
tance, and He will bring alignment. He'll bring a grace

and a refreshing upon you, because He knows you're at your best when you're lined up with the pattern He's laid out for you. Nothing shows us greater success in this endeavor than the life and ministry of Jesus. He is our heavenly pattern. We don't have to figure this out; the work has already been done for us.

www.ingramcontent.com/pod-product-compliance
Lightning Source LLC
Chambersburg PA
CBHW030835090426
42737CB00009B/986